The Savvy Do Gooder
Giving that Makes a Difference

―❦―

By Nadine Riopel

With foreword by Tad Hargrave

The Savvy Do Gooder: Giving that Makes a Difference

© 2012 Nadine Riopel. All rights reserved.

ISBN 978-0-9916894-0-8

Cover design by Karin Locke

For Glyn –
for being the best lifetime teammate
anyone could ever hope to have.

Table of Contents

Foreword 7

Introduction 13
    THE TALE OF THE WORN-OUT DO GOODER

Chapter 1 20
    THE STORY OF MY DEEPEST WOUND

Chapter 2 33
    THE FIRST STEP: IDENTIFY THE CHANGE
    YOU WANT TO SEE IN THE WORLD

Chapter 3 48
    THE SECOND STEP: UNDERSTAND YOUR ISSUE

Chapter 4 62
    THE THIRD STEP: PICK THE RIGHT PARTNER

Chapter 5 73
    THE FOURTH STEP: BUILD YOUR RELATIONSHIPS

Conclusion 81

Foreword

By Tad Hargrave, Marketing for Hippies

My friend and colleague Nadine Riopel has written a book about doing good in the world.

And that's something the world needs a lot more of.

Of course that word 'more' is a bit of a problem. Because there's always 'more' to do.

And if there's always more to do and we can't do it all ... then what on Earth should we do? And how do we decide?

This is the question Nadine raises for us.

I think most of us end up choosing where to give by default. We choose what's in our face and convenient; we jump on the trendy movement of the moment; we do what our friends are doing.

And we often do it out of a sense of obligation, guilt or a desire for us to feel a little 'more' inside.

The desire to contribute and give is real. And yet I don't think most of us really ever feel the satisfaction of having given fully.

There are two main issues addressed in this book.

The first is: how can we really have an impact? How can we not only be 'do gooders' but savvy do gooders? How can we make sure that our life's energy, time and money doesn't just produce a lot of movement, but actually helps build a movement? Not just busy work, but lasting results that leave the world better than we found it.

The second issue is about our own happiness.

I remember when I was a child bringing my mom breakfast in bed. I carried the tray in, and it's hard to know whose smile was bigger: mine for the pride I felt making my mom so happy, or hers out of pride in me. But it's one of my earliest memories of really getting it - that giving to others feels good.

We are not truly happy until we have found a way to give our gifts to the world. No one wants to die with their music still inside of them.

*

It's 1998. I'm sitting at a University class at Berkeley. And a young student is standing up, chastising Hollywood actor Woody Harrelson to his face as he attempts to address the class.

"When are you going to get on the streets and do the real work ... with the people?!"

This is really happening.

The student gets applause from the others seated there.

Woody seems sad. He's doing his best. He's showing up to share his experience with the students ... and he's being criticized for it instead of celebrated for it.

Of course, this happens a lot.

And it needs to stop.

In her book, The Great Turning, Joanna Macy shared her notion that there are three major types of work we need to see in the world to make sure these times are known as the Great Turning and not the Great Unraveling.

The first kind of work she called Holding Actions: tree sits, lockdowns, protests, letters to the editor, direct action, etc. Anything that tried to draw attention to and slow down the juggernaut of destruction.

The second kind of work she called Alternatives: straw bale, compact fluorescent light bulbs, permaculture, local food, local currencies, barter, etc. Anything that created other, more sustainable and beautiful, ways for us to get our needs met.

The third kind of work she called Shifting Consciousness: the work of the Deep Ecology movement fits here, decolonization, healing. This is the work where we unlearn all the things that have us hurting each other and the world around us.

Her point was that we need all three of these. That without all three, we will certainly see the unraveling of everything we hold dear.

And yet, instead of a celebration of these different elements of and approaches to positive change in the world, we often see a criticism of each other. We see people trying to claim a monopoly on the 'real work'.

Activists tell you that the real work is out on the streets doing direct actions. They remind you that great power has never conceded anything without a fight.

People engaged in local food alternatives turn up their noses and say,

"Your poorly organized anarchist protests are nice. But where are you going to get your food if this system collapses? What are you actually adding to the world besides your complaining?"

And people engaged in the work of shifting consciousness just shake their heads and say, "Unless you heal this in your heart you'll just recreate what you don't want in your efforts. The real work is inside."

But why can't it all be real work? Why can't it all be important? Instead of obsessing about which work is the most real or true - why don't we each just look at the contribution that is the best fit for us personally?

And instead of criticizing people doing a different kind of work, why can't we look for ways to collaborate with them and support them? Why don't we see them as mutually reinforcing and vital?

Why can't we be grateful for the fact that there are some many different ways to do good and that other people are drawn to doing the things we aren't?

Instead of people being drawn to doing different kinds of work causing us grief ... maybe it should be a cause of relief.

As my friend Jennifer Corriero says, "is the fact that we all approach making positive change differently tragic? ... or is it magic?"

*

It's the year 2000. The Battle in Seattle has energized the activist movement globally. We're seeing huge rallies with hundreds of people around issues of multinational corporate globalization. I'm at another protest that starts at Edmonton's Gazebo Park and moves down, across the bridge to Ezio Farraone Park. There's such an amazing energy in the air. I walk up to the Gazebo and see two of my friends, young women, leading some chants on the megaphones. They seem really uncomfortable doing it. I go up and give them hugs and ask if I can help in any way.

They immediately shove the bullhorn into my hands with a pleading look in their eyes that says, "please take this over - we don't want to do this".

We speak afterwards and one of them says, "I just want to collect soil samples. I only do the protests because I think I should. It seems like the cool thing to be doing but I really just love being out in nature."

And it's like this for a lot of us. We're contributing to the world but not in a way that feels best for us. Not in a way that really uses our core strengths and gifts and passions.

Fast forward one year and the protests are small. I'm walking by the Gazebo and I see a poorly organized rally where the only people present are the organizers. They're preaching to the converted. Or they would ... but they've also forgotten their sound system.

Somehow, within a year, we went from huge rallies back to almost nothing. The movement feels discouraged. And I think it's got a lot to do with how no one gathered emails during the rallies, no one developed leadership; how there was little education given and action taken on those days where so many people were gathered.

A rally is a powerful moment. It can do so much and have such impact when done well but when it's poorly organized, it does so much less.

Meanwhile, what Nadine is inviting us to do is do more with less.

You have limited time in your life. Limited energy. How do you want to spend it that will have the most genuine impact and make you the happiest?

And I think to do this we need to slow down.

There's the Slow Food, Slow Fashion, Slow Sex movements ... how about a Slow Do Gooding movement where, instead of panicking out of a desperate desire to 'do something', we slow down, step back and find the sweet spot where our gifts meet the needs in the world? Maybe we do fewer things, but we do them better. We collaborate more with people who can help us in areas we're weak.

In their article, "Action Will Be Taken": Left Anti-intellectualism and Its Discontents, Liza Featherstone, Doug Henwood, and Christian Parenti share their observation that activists had come to a place where they were practicing not activism but actionism - the need to take action. Instead of thinking about big picture strategy on how to create an impact, all that's thought of are the tactics to employ: throw another rally, donate more money, volunteer more hours.

More.

Always more.

*

I'm sitting in Chiang Mai, Thailand at a sustainable living center called Pun Pun. It's a gathering of thirty young changemakers from around the world (ages 20 - 40). We are spending the week sharing the stories of our work and getting to know each other. And one day it strikes me how hard we all are on ourselves. This feeling that we're not doing enough. And it blows my mind. If anyone on the planet should be let off the hook for not doing enough, it would be these incredibly accomplished movement leaders and changemakers. But even they feel this sense of shame and beat themselves up for all the 'more' that they could be doing.

When mainstream America feels inadequate inside, they go shopping.

When do gooders feel inadequate, they take on another project. They do a little more.

If we do more good, then surely we're a better person ... right?

I think so much 'do gooding' is motivated by not feeling like we're enough. The belief if we just do that one more good thing, we'll be worthy of love - from others, ourselves ... and even God.

But maybe we're not here to earn God's love. Maybe we're here to spend it.

And Nadine's book is here to help you spend it wisely.

Introduction

THE TALE OF THE WORN-OUT DO GOODER

It's a grey afternoon in mid-November. You're at work. The hot dog you had at noon left you hungry, but you didn't have the heart to bring your own lunch, when the social committee worked so hard on a fundraising BBQ for victims of the latest major international disaster. Your voicemail light is flashing. You know it's your friend calling to see if you've asked your boss about sponsoring his hockey team yet, and you're dodging him.

On the other side of the desk, the donation package that appeared there last week lurks, with its colourful brochures and persuasive arguments about having money taken off your paycheque every week to feed the hungry or house the homeless or... something.

Finally it's quitting time, so you grab your coat and get in the car. By now, you've passed the billboards on your way so often, you're numb to their loud messages about how much your help is needed for a number of good causes.

Stopping at the grocery store, you walk by the shelf of conveniently packaged items you're invited to buy for the local food bank, and grab the milk and bananas you came for; also bypassing the raft of pink items that promise to cure breast cancer if only you'd just buy them. While you're paying, the cashier asks if you'd like to add a dollar to your bill for a firefighters' relief fund. You give in. Why not? It's only a dollar. On your way out, you try not to catch the eye of the sweet-looking elderly woman selling raffle tickets for the children's hospital.

Home at last, you get the mail on your way in. There are two fliers for charity home lotteries, and three envelopes actually addressed to you. Two of those are bills. The third is from a local shelter you vaguely remember volunteering at for a holiday meal a few years back. It's a letter about the growing need and a pre-addressed envelope for you to send money in.

Once inside, you check your messages, one of which is your sister asking if you wouldn't mind buying a coupon book for her kids' school fundraiser. You'll think about it later. Right now, you need a bite to eat. Just as you're sitting down, the phone rings. It's an anti-bullying campaigner wanting to know if they can count on your support. Before you say anything, they launch into a five-minute monologue about the evils of bullying, and suggest a $100 donation. You refuse, since you really don't know much about it. They counter-offer $75. This continues until they get to $20 and you finally agree. After all, bullying is bad, and what's $20, right? It's worth it just to get back to your dinner.

After eating, you sit down to watch some TV and almost immediately, you're bombarded with images of starving children, and sad-faced celebrities telling you in hushed tones that you're their best hope for a better life; please send money now. You feel for these children, but it occurs to you that something's familiar about the logo; you've given money to it every year for the past 3 years. By the looks of the commercial, it's not helping much. You remember having gotten another request for money from them recently, but can't recall ever seeing any information about how it's being spent or if it's making any difference.

The news comes on, and the lead story is about the director of a famous national charitable organization who's been sacked for embezzling and mismanagement, and is now facing criminal charges. The organization's donors are up in arms, demanding justice, feeling betrayed.

Does any of this sound familiar? The average person has experienced most, if not all, of these things in the course of their daily life. Hopefully, you've never had to actually deal with all of them in a single day, but it's not outside the realm of possibility in the world we live in; a world where fundraising and engagement campaigns have reached a fever pitch. It can seem like everyone wants a piece of you, and no matter how much you give of your time, money and talent , it's never enough. You may get a "thank you", but the next thing you know, you're being asked for more.

And what good is it doing? Too often, we don't know. With this amount of fundraising happening, you'd think that evidence of the good it's doing would be everywhere. But even the people asking for the money often have only the most superficial understanding of the organization they're doing it for. The next time you're asked to give to something at the checkout of your grocery or drug store, try asking the cashier what he or she knows about the organization it's going to. I'm willing to bet that the answer will be: not much.

So what's the point? Why do we participate in any of it? Why do we put up with it? All this noisy clamouring for our money, our time, our attention; our blood; is at best a nuisance, and at worst a terrible betrayal.

It bothers us because we care: our beautiful humanity

The answer lies in the most fundamental building blocks of our humanity. Deep down, we all want to do good. It's that simple. We want to make a meaningful contribution to the world we live in. When we see suffering or injustice, we can't help but want to do something about it. By the same token, when we see opportunities to make things better, we're drawn to them.

This is a wonderful, beautiful thing. This is what builds community and family. There's love in it. It's noble. If everyone in the world could fully realize the drive to do good that lives within each of us, wouldn't it be a much better place?

That's why we don't simply tune out the endless requests for us to 'get involved', 'get active', 'make a difference' and 'give back'. They inspire feelings of guilt, pressure and resentment because deep down, we really do want to do those things. The reason that it bothers us is that we care, and the more we care, the more it bothers us.

We're affected because we know that charity appeals are a manifestation of someone else's drive to do good, and that speaks to us. We're bothered because at some level, we don't feel that we're doing enough good ourselves. If we did, the appeals wouldn't have any power over us. If you're a person who is confident in the knowledge that you're making the best possible contribution to the world, you'll feel perfectly at ease opting out of the whole fundraising frenzy. It just won't register.

You can feel better and do more good

If you can find the path that works best for you according to your resources and your values, there's no reason for you to pay attention to any of the rest. You will have regained control over your giving. You will have taken the power away from those who manipulate your noble instincts; as if the choice were between giving to everything, and being a bad person.

You'll be able to focus on the healthy and rewarding process of making your giving really work; you'll be someone who understands the impact you're trying make, understands your role in making it happen, and (perhaps best of all) understands the results of what you're doing. You will be a Savvy Do Gooder.

That kind of a giver is the key to turning good intentions into real positive change. Savvy Do Gooders are the best way to get the maximum amount of good out of the charitable sector. A charity can only be as well run, focused, and effective as its supporters enable it to be.

The questions that supporters ask most are the questions charities come up with the answers for. The things the supporters hold the charities accountable for are the things the charities focus on and measure. The tactics that attract supporters are the ones the charities keep doing. The ones that make them walk away get dropped pretty quickly. Activities that can get funded get done, and ones that can't never see the light of day.

As an individual, you have the potential to have enormous influence over how much good is accomplished, if you approach it in a savvy, proactive way. Doing good is not about charities. It's about you. Charities only exist as a vehicle for you to do the good that you crave deep down. They are tools for good, and they're not the only ones. Choosing the right tool and using it correctly is your best strategy for making a difference.

You're more powerful than you think

You might be thinking,

"Sure, whatever – I'm just one person with a little bit of money. What about big companies and government? They give millions. They must have more influence than me."

It's true that companies and governments are major contributors to charity, but here's the thing: when it comes to causes, you control them, too.

In the case of government, the proof of this is obvious. Governments work for the people. The bosses of government are elected officials, responsible to the general public, which includes you. It's not a perfect system, but public opinion does have a huge impact on how governments behave, and that includes how they work with the charities our tax dollars fund.

Our control over the charitable behaviour of corporations is less obvious, but it became clear to me during a recent conference.

I'll never forget the experience I had at the Western Sponsorship Congress in Calgary, Alberta in the fall of 2011. The event was populated mainly by two kinds of people; corporate sponsorship folks talking about what it was going to take to get a piece of their financial pie; and people who wanted that money – everyone from charities to sports teams to municipalities.

There was a lot of interesting discussion, but what stuck out like a sore thumb for me was the complete absence of any mention of the impact of all this activity. Nobody said one word about selecting things to sponsor based on how much good they could do. Some of the charity representatives, when I asked, admitted they were a bit uncomfortable about the lack of impact discussion, but they said it in a whisper, as if they were afraid of being heard.

This seemed profoundly weird to me. Luckily, I was not there representing anyone but myself, so I had no fears about speaking up. I asked some of the corporate sponsorship people about it, and what I heard was amazing.

Their perspective is that they have a mandate to make money. Everything they do is in service of that goal, including sponsorship and giving.[1] Setting social policy is not their role. Deciding which charities, or even which causes, are most deserving is not their job. They are giving to look good to two groups; employees and customers. This impacts their bottom line by making recruitment, sales, and human resource management easier.

With that in mind, they make sponsorship and giving decisions based on which causes and organizations are most important to employees and customers. The decisions are entirely up to those people, whether they realize it or not. Their opinions ultimately determine where all that corporate money ends up.

And who are those people? Us. We are the workforce and the customer base. If you're a student, you're an even more desirable target, because you're the workforce and the customer base of the future.

Don't underestimate your power in this area. You don't have to be a major donor with big bucks. You don't have to be a huge corporation with its name on a sports arena. You, personally, really do have the power to change the world.

That's why I wrote this book for you, the Savvy Do Gooder, instead of for the charities or the companies or the government.

Many people have said to me,
"If you want to improve the way good is done, wouldn't it make sense to work with the charities?"

Or,
"You should work with corporations – they're always trying to figure out how to manage their Corporate Social Responsibility stuff."

That never felt right to me. I know now it's because ultimately, doing good is about regular people like you and me. The drive,

---

[1] I don't necessarily agree with this point of view, but it seems to be a pretty common one in the corporate world.

the passion, the pure and beautiful need to help – it comes from within each of us.

Everything else is just an expression of that drive. It's not about them. They work for us. As big and powerful as charities, companies and governments may be, they're simply the vehicles we use to get to where we want to go.

If we want them to do a better job of that and do more good, it has to start with us.

So - let's get started.

1

*I always wondered why somebody
didn't do something about that.
Then I realized, I am somebody.*

- *Graffiti found on the Internet*

THE STORY OF MY DEEPEST WOUND

Tad Hargrave of Marketing for Hippies is one of my favourite gurus on the subject of becoming successful doing what you love to do. "Your deepest wound is your truest niche" is one of his favourite sayings. What I take it to mean is:

The people we're best suited to serve in our work are the people who are experiencing pain we've felt ourselves.

In the course of my life so far, I've discovered this is as true of me as anyone else. I understand the pain of wanting to do good but feeling blocked in that for many, many years. I've come at it from several angles, experiencing little victories and little failures, and learning all the way.

Here's the story of how it all went down (so far).

My original passion

For most of my adult life, I've felt driven to fight suffering; to try to make the world a better place. As a student, I studied history, geography, politics and languages in the hopes of becoming a diplomat. I kept pictures of drought, land mine, and abuse victims on my computer desktop as a motivating reminder of what I really wanted; to fight against unacceptable conditions that lead to such suffering.

For 2 years, I was part of a university student volunteer group that sponsored refugee students to immigrate to Canada and attend our school. During my tenure, we sponsored a young man from Sudan and a woman from Burma/Myanmar.

Volunteer struggles

Despite our best efforts, the refugee sponsorships never turned out very well. The young man behaved inappropriately in response to my attempts to welcome him, and refused to accept it when his year of financial support was up. One day, I took him on a tour of the city, showed him how to grocery shop, and how to make a sandwich. Not long after, I started receiving long love letters from him via email. Maybe in the Sudanese culture, showing someone how to make a sandwich is a declaration of love. Maybe for a motherless boy who grew up surrounded by other boys in a war zone, this kind of hospitality seemed like more than it was. Maybe to someone accustomed to surviving on foreign aid, the idea that the handouts were over was impossible to deal with. Either way, it was clear that my group and I were not equipped to deal with the emotional and cultural fallout of his move to Canada.

The young woman turned out to be pregnant, insisted on having her baby's father sponsored as well, and when they arrived, she was completely unhappy with the accommodations we had worked so hard to prepare for them. We had spent months arranging to rent and furnish an apartment big enough for a mother and child, while every update from Myanmar contradicted or changed the information we had. Once the student, her baby, and the father finally arrived, they were bitterly and vocally disappointed with the furnished 2 bedroom apartment near campus. At the time, we felt they were ungrateful, but I'm sure the truth was more complex than that. To this day, I don't understand everything that went on in the process of our attempt to help them, and I probably never will.

Despite the fact that the parent organization of our group was headquartered in the same city as our school, we couldn't get the right support to deal with these challenges. There was little or no help for us to deal with the non-material needs of our sponsored students. They did not seem to be able to do anything about communication problems with students who hadn't yet arrived, or about constant changes to the plan. There were very few employees, they always seemed to be overloaded, and there was a lot of staff turnover.

So we muddled along as best we could, making changes where we could, making our excuses for the things the refugees were unhappy about that we couldn't change, and watching the relationships sour. Nevertheless, the results of our efforts were not the cheerful, grateful, self-sufficient new citizens we had envisioned. I honestly don't know where either of the sponsored students are today – sadly, neither case led to a sustainable relationship. When I think of the experience, I still feel stung and regretful.

What was wrong, in hindsight

In retrospect, I can see what went wrong. As young university students, we were woefully under qualified to provide support for refugees. We came from a world of stable government, clean water, and no war. They came from worlds where water is never clean, government is never to be trusted, and conflict is an ever-present threat. Sure - we could fundraise, rent apartments, and show them around town. But the support that a refugee needs to move past years of trauma and adapt to an entirely new environment goes far beyond that. We were out of our depth.

Meanwhile, the charitable organization that was supposed to be managing all this was operating on a shoestring budget; under-resourced and overly ambitious. They had a beautiful mission, but no ability to execute on it in a consistently high-quality way. As a result, my committee and I struggled, we were frustrated, and we achieved disappointing results.

This was my first experience of having something that inspired grand ideas of 'helping' and 'saving' people fall short of my expectations; of something that convinced me that volunteering would lead to my 'making a difference', but just didn't deliver. At the time, I chalked it up to that particular organization being poorly run.

I didn't become disillusioned about volunteering - I had also had a good experience at the same school organizing a collection drive within the student residences for a charity thrift shop. At the end of my first year in the dorms, I was amazed to see giant dumpsters rolled into the residence courtyard, and filled up with all the "junk" that the students had bought over the course of the year, but that wasn't going to fit into their suitcases or their cars for the journey home for the summer. There were sad little piles of this stuff in the dormitory hallways, with signs reading, "Still good – please take!"

Now, I'm genetically predisposed to hate waste (I'm told I get this from my Scot grandmother). So this state of affairs was, to me, untenable. I started thinking – how could I find a way to get all this stuff to people who could use it? I ended up phoning, then visiting, the local charity thrift shop. I found out that they took donations of resalable items, sold them in their thrift stores, and used the proceeds to help people with barriers to employment get back into the workforce. They were willing to take the unwanted stuff.

The next year, things were different. I had drop locations set up in every residence building, and pickup dates arranged with the thrift shop people. The drop boxes soon filled to overflowing, and my friends and I were kept very busy putting everything into plastic trash bags for pickup. In the end, we filled a very large delivery truck with donations. It was the first year of what would become an annual collection drive. The students had somewhere to put their unwanted things, the university saved on waste disposal, and the thrift shop got a large quantity of stuff to sell to fuel their work. It was a win-win-win.

So when it came to the mixed results of my attempt at saving refugees, I just wrote off that particular experience and carried on working towards my goal of creating social change.

A dose of reality

During my time at university, my dream was to become a diplomat. I had grand visions of travelling the world resolving conflict, improving international cooperation, and other such laudable activities.

A combination of; participation in events at the Department of Foreign Affairs and International Trade; the application process for the service; and international relations classes eventually disabused me of this notion. By the time I graduated, I realized that the diplomatic service was far too political and bureaucratic for my burning idealism.

My second choice was the non-profit world; Amnesty International, the Red Cross, Doctors Without Borders, here I came!

I spent my final semester on exchange in Mexico. I went as part of a NAFTA scholarship. For a young woman hoping to work in the field of international aid and development, a student exchange program seemed like the perfect choice. I was able to develop my schoolbook Spanish into fluency, and I learned a lot; most of it outside the classroom. Living in an environment and a culture so completely foreign to anything I was used to was an incredibly valuable experience. But it also meant that graduation found me back in my hometown of Edmonton; weak from a long and severe bout of food poisoning, and with few resources.

There aren't many international Non Governmental Organizations (NGOs) headquartered in Edmonton, and it soon became apparent my ideal employers didn't hire entry-level staff from the other side of the country, no matter how enthusiastic. None of the resumes I hopefully sent garnered even a phone call in return. So I investigated international volunteering options, hoping to find an opportunity to earn some experience, even if it didn't pay much.

Another harsh lesson was in store for me: most volunteer opportunities for recent graduates not only don't pay; they actually require payment to participate. Broke as I was, this wasn't an option.

So I bit the bullet and took work in offices answering phones and taking minutes; not much different from what I'd done before going back to school. But I remained determined to get back into the business of world-changing as soon as possible, so I started looking for volunteer opportunities I could do on the side.

The rocky road of volunteering

Over the course of the next few years, I attempted to volunteer for at least three different organizations; a large local charity; a small international charity headquartered locally; and the local branch of a large international charity.

All three expressed enthusiasm to have me on board. All three invited me to various meetings and events. One of them sent me to several training courses.

But none of them ever actually put me to good use. In spite of numerous conversations about how I might help; in spite of my continuing to show up to whatever I was invited to; in spite of the fact that my education, skills and interests were well matched to the missions of all three, I never truly believed that I was making a contribution that mattered.

Only one of the organizations gave me concrete tasks, and they were pretty obviously make-work: The ESL classes I taught were empty from the start. The at-risk kids I was supposed to be tutoring rarely showed up, and were unenthusiastic when they did. Most days, the only one who came was a young boy who actually lived in the building, in a subsidized housing unit owned by the organization, and the volunteer coordinator usually had to go drag him out of his apartment to come and receive my generous 'help'.

The feedback I got from my staff contacts was unfailingly positive but I could tell that my work was not making a meaningful difference to anyone. There was plainly a disconnect between my desire to help and their ability to use that help. My frustration increased.

One by one, I dropped all my volunteer commitments; sometimes after over a year of trying to make it work.

A turn for the better

The first positive volunteer experience I had in Edmonton finally came about through my job. I was working as an executive assistant for a large company when the management decided to run their first campaign with an organization that campaigns for several local charities.

This was something different. The expectations for a campaign committee member were clear. I was able to plunge into the role of education coordinator, organizing multiple presentations about the charities' work.

This began my love affair with education as a fundraising tactic. I believed then, as now, that giving people meaningful information about how their money is used is the most respectful and foolproof way to win support. It was a very rewarding experience. I liked the due diligence being done to invest donations wisely. I felt like what I was doing had value.

When I decided to leave the company, I was recruited by the organization to be one of their campaign managers, and thus began my career as a 'resource development professional' (aka fundraiser and volunteer manager, in my case).

The honeymoon period with a good organization

I found being a campaign manager very rewarding at first. There's a lot I like about the organization's approach to community building; especially the research and evaluation done on the organizations and initiatives that receive funds. Every year, they organize groups of volunteers and professional evaluators to visit the funded charities and make sure that the money was being well spent. They work very collaboratively with the funded charities to find ways to tackle big problems better. Often, they play a role in bringing different groups together to work on specific initiatives, like ending homelessness.

The problems that started to bother me after a while were not unique to the organization I worked for. I still believe it's a good organization as charities go, but it's affected by the same issues as most.

Resistant and misinformed 'supporters'

On hearing I worked for a charity, most people had one of two reactions. Some responded with enthusiastic praise. Others became uncomfortable and cagey, as if they expected me to pressure them for money on the spot.

Some of the volunteers from the companies that supported us who were assigned to work with me were enthusiastic and open. Most weren't. They made excuses, argued with everything I suggested, didn't return phone calls or email, and broke promises. I spent a lot of my time as a professional campaigner chasing these people. Remember: these were representatives of companies who had said 'yes' to participating in the campaigns, not of new companies we were trying to convince.

I also noticed that in spite of the organization's decades of history, professional marketing and communications department, and armies of staff and volunteers deployed annually to promote it, almost no one I met actually had any idea what the organization did. In talking to people I met in the community, and even with my own family, I found over and over that, while people knew the organization's name, they could not provide even a basic explanation of its work. Even my big boss, the executive director, was well aware of this, often saying, "We're well known, but we're not known well." This was very frustrating, as I spent all my time explaining just that with speeches, brochures, one-on-one conversations, and more. If we had spent over 65 years spreading the word, why wasn't it working?

The value/action disconnect

Disconnects between the official messaging I was delivering and the reality I was seeing began to bother me. We said we were at the core of a movement whose true drivers were community members. But from where I sat, it looked like there were very few non-staff members who did anything without the impetus and control of the organization. We said we wanted volunteer input and direction, but rarely seemed to make any significant changes based on what they told us. Volunteers who made speeches were usually scripted and coached by staff.

We claimed to respect any informed decision about whether to support us, but if a major donor or big company decided to stop, it was full-court press. We called, we emailed, we showed up. We had repeated conversations about why they didn't want to be on our team anymore. We searched our list of contacts for someone who might be able to get them to change their minds. We asked our volunteers to do the same.

I once had a company stop running campaigns because their Toronto head office decreed a different organization as their charity of choice. The local management did their best to be allowed to continue with us, but failed. It reached a point where the local folks' jobs were in danger if they did not drop us. It wasn't their fault; they had done their best.

And yet, it was over a year before my fellow staff members stopped insisting there must be some other angle we could try, someone else we could call, pushing me to go back and try again. We did not give up easy, even when the 'no' was clearly and respectfully given. No wonder so many chose to dodge us instead.

I remember a volunteer saying that once we had someone's contact info, they could never escape. It was said half in jest, but there was truth in it, and even a little bitterness.

I'll never forget the time I sat with our volunteer representative for a large company while she ripped me up one side and down the other. She was so angry. A lot of her arguments were based on misinformation. She was simultaneously enraged that we were too big, and that we did not fund every charity in town. She clearly didn't understand our discriminating model based on evaluation and collaboration. But that just proves my earlier point - how could even those officially representing our organization to hundreds of their coworkers be so grossly misinformed, and feel so alienated?

I noticed that although we managed by hook or by crook to raise more total dollars every year, the number of donors had been steadily declining for years. People were voting with their feet. Our 'movement' was shrinking.

The beginning of my enlightenment

Meanwhile, I was learning new things. I participated in a session on sales skills by Linda Maul of Creating People Power[2] that radically shifted my views on donor relations. I was reading a lot

---

[2] Creating People Power, http://www.creatingpeoplepower.ca/
[July 31, 2012]

- people like Penelope Burk[3] (who promotes the idea of donor-centered fundraising) and Richard Harwood[4] (who believes the community organizers must shift their focus from their organizations to the people around them – an outward orientation). I started to realize there were new ideas that could be applied to our situation; that might improve our image and increase our effectiveness.

I began to see a different way of doing things, a way that would involve our supporters in more meaningful ways and put more focus on their experience. I wanted to focus the fundraising more on the donor, not the dollar. I wanted to stop talking about us and start talking about them. I wanted to ask people what they wanted from us, even if we weren't sure we would be able to give them everything we heard. I wanted to start giving volunteers different kinds of tasks, like making thank-you calls to other supporters, even if it meant us losing a bit of control over our message. I wanted to take control of that message out of the hands of the professional marketers and put it into the hands of the community. 65 years of professionally crafted messaging hadn't gotten us much real understanding – what if we got a little messy with it?

I began to agitate for some of these things. Superficially, I was encouraged. It wasn't that the leadership didn't want to be open to new things, and they were well aware that there was room for improvement. But there were practical and philosophical factors that made big change very difficult.

For me, things were destined to get worse.

Caution we can't afford

Change is difficult in any environment. But it seemed to me that at the organization I worked for, it was harder than it needed to be. This was reinforced for me by reading about how things

---

[3] Cygnus Applied Research, Inc.,
http://www.cygresearch.com/pb/?gclid=CLqI4MfmxLECFSgbQg odVEkAnw [July 31, 2012]
[4] The Harwood Institute,
http://www.theharwoodinstitute.org/index.php?ht=d/sp/i/1299 9/pid/12999 [July 31, 2012]

could be, and my experiences on the ground of community fundraising. I saw firsthand how our inability to adapt was negatively impacting our ability to deliver on our mission.

Listening to front line workers from the organizations we supported, I could also see how little room for waste there was in this work; how important it was that we excel at the job of rallying community members to build a better place for us all to live in.

One experience that stands out is a speech by the executive director of a local youth shelter. She'd been running it for decades, right down in the trenches. She's a tough lady, but she was moved to tears as she explained how our city had become a hub for international human trafficking, and how young escapees or rejects from that hideous trade often end up at her shelter.

This is the kind of thing that motivated me, as a campaigner, to do a better job.

The barriers to change

I wanted to implement new things I was reading about and eliminate others that I could see were costing us supporters. And that's where I often hit a wall.

I was never told my ideas were bad, exactly. There was just a lot of resistance to implementing them, for a variety of reasons. Some examples:

- Changing the software to make the admin side of volunteering less painful: too complicated, too expensive, too risky
- Offering volunteers additional tasks, such as making thank-you calls to donors: too risky
- Translating materials into other languages for workplace campaigns with a lot of non-English speakers: too expensive, too difficult, too risky

The harder I pushed, the less popular I became. Have patience, they said. Be more diplomatic, they said. To their credit, they've now implemented some of these things, but for me it was too little, too late. It breaks my heart to think of the opportunity cost of the time we spent delaying these positive changes.

I'll be the first to admit that I can be a little intense. But after three years of running up against the same obstacles, hearing a lot of talk about change, and seeing it happen at a snail's pace if at all, I was pretty sure the problem wasn't all me.

The system is broken

And after a decade of unsatisfactory attempts to make a positive impact on this world, after having tried to come at it as a diplomat, a volunteer, and a charity employee, I was beginning to believe the system was broken.

Based on my reading of the experts and my conversations with other charity employees, I knew that this resistance to anything expensive or risky or fast was pretty much universal in the sector.

Based on my fundraising work, on media coverage of the sector, and on comments in public forums, I also knew that others shared my frustration.

I came to believe that there's a huge gap between the experts calling for the sector to progress and the donors and volunteers whose opinions and behaviour have such enormous influence over how it operates. I became extremely passionate about bridging that gap.

What drives my passion today

I've discovered that there is a better way to give, and the path to it is actually easier and more enjoyable than the way most people are doing it. The kicker is this: the more enjoyable path is also the one that leads to more good being done.

Now, I'm working to bring this information to as many people as possible. I want people to question the old methods and rules our society has built up around doing good, rejecting those that aren't working anymore. There's no real basis to ideas like: doing good must be completely selfless; low-cost organizations are more worthy of support, and; the more charities you give to, the better.

I want people to embrace instead the things that are going to work best for each of them according to what they, personally, want to accomplish.

This book is a part of that; a step-by-step guide to take people from a place of frustration, of darkness, of powerlessness; to a place of confidence, of light, of knowledge, of empowerment and satisfaction. It's also a part of the same journey for me.

I started out trying to play by the rules; supporting whatever charity would have me; asking about admin costs instead of looking for a good fit; pretending that what I needed from the situation was irrelevant; and found that those rules simply didn't work for me. As I learned more about the space I was working in, I discovered that I was going to have to buck the trends and go my own way. It's been a long journey, but I've learned a lot along the way.

And now, I know I've found my path whenever; I see relief in the face of someone realizing they don't have to follow limiting old social 'rules' about doing good; I see shock in the face of someone realizing for the first time that they deserve more from their giving; and every time someone thanks me for helping them discover a path that feels right.

2

I am only one.
I cannot do everything, but I can still do something.
And because I cannot do everything, I will not refuse
to do the something I can do.

- Helen Keller

THE FIRST STEP: IDENTIFY THE CHANGE YOU WANT TO SEE IN THE WORLD

Mahatma Ghandi famously said,

"Be the change you want to see in the world."

It's a beautiful sentiment. The problem with it, in my view, is that it skips a very important step. Before we can 'be' anything, we need to know what change it is we want to see in the world.

If we don't know where we're hoping to go, how will we know when we get there?

If we don't know what our goal is, how will we be able to hold charities (or even ourselves) accountable for progress?

I've often had this problem myself. For example, when I was fundraising professionally, I never got the same sense of fulfillment from participating in hands-on work that others seemed to. I would go to a food hamper-stuffing workshop and come away feeling unfulfilled. I also felt guilty, because others seemed to find it so rewarding. I didn't know what was the matter with me.

Turns out, I was deflated because the change I'm really passionate about is for charity to be more effective as a system. Spending an afternoon in a food bank warehouse does not do that for me. It's not filling food hampers is a bad thing, but it's the wrong thing for me. So putting my time and energy into it left me feeling cheated.

Meanwhile, if I ever got the chance to attend an evaluation meeting with an organization we were funding, I came away totally jazzed! I had been a part of working on improving relationships and structures that made the whole system go. I had contributed to the process of making giving smarter. Woo hoo! Bring it on! So satisfying.

Once I discovered this about myself and became a full-blown charity nerd (leaving the hands-on work to people who thrive on it), everything started to work better for me. My involvement became much more rewarding. Finding the right fit for me made all the difference.

Not knowing what results we're hoping to produce sets us up for failure and disappointment. It's very unfair to do this to ourselves. And it doesn't help the charity either, for that matter. Without a clear sense of what you're hoping for, you don't have anywhere to go when the things you try disappoint you.

It's often assumed that we automatically know what the best fit is for us; and that we have everything we need to make that decision. As I mentioned in the Introduction, even the companies we work for and buy from take their giving cues from us, assuming that we've got it all figured out. But it's not that easy, is it?

There are a lot of good causes out there; each more compelling than the last. It can be very difficult to sort them out and choose which ones to support with our time and money.

They're all worthwhile

Let's get something clear right off the bat: almost all causes are good causes. I often hear people promoting an issue or defending their choice to support one by saying,

"It's a really good cause."

This statement is meaningless, because there is almost no such thing as a bad cause. If something can accurately be called a 'cause' in the context of giving, chances are that it's a good one. Whether something is worthwhile or deserving of support depends to some degree on your point of view, so there are a few causes whose merit is debatable (like pro-life and pro-choice movements, for example), but most of them are above reproach.

Few people would argue that things like education, ending poverty, curing disease, or international development are in any way bad. What are questionable are the specific approaches to those causes.

You might agree that fighting poverty is a good cause, but not support a strategy that calls for giving low-income children $50 cash each every day. You might agree that reducing overpopulation is a worthwhile goal, but not be on board with mass sterilization of young women.

The causes behind these sketchy tactics, though, are not in question. Most causes are good.

That's why worthiness of a cause should not play a role in your decision of whether to support it or not. There is no 'right' or 'best' cause. There is, however, a right cause for you, and the purpose of this chapter is to help you discover what that is.

You're going to have to pick one

At this point, you might be asking yourself,

"What do you mean, 'right cause'; singular? Are you saying I have to pick just one?"

Yes, I'm afraid I am. I strongly believe that the more causes you attempt to impact, the less impact you will actually have on each of them. That's why ideally (and especially at first) you should cut your giving back to just one cause.

I know this is hard. I understand that you've probably been interacting with charities and causes since you were a tiny tot, and have pre-existing ties that will be hard to cut. I get that you have probably been personally touched by more than one issue in your life.

It might help to note that I'm not recommending you restrict yourself to one organization, necessarily, just one issue.

I'm also not saying you have to choose one issue for life. It's not a good idea to change causes as often as toothbrushes, but you don't have to stick with the same one forever. Time passes, priorities change. You may spend a few years working to bring about a certain kind of change, then move on to something else. But it does make sense to focus on one issue at a time, and commit to it for long enough to make a valuable contribution.

The reason I feel this way is illustrated in the old saying,

"Jack of all trades, master of none."

The good we hope to accomplish through giving is complex and difficult. If homelessness and hunger and political injustice and disease had quick fixes, they would be fixed by now. It's hard enough to make a difference in one area, never mind several.

Focus will help you do more good

Have you ever had someone try to help you who didn't really know you? Ever met someone and shared a problem with them, only to have them start spitting out advice about how to solve it five minutes later? It's not usually very good advice, is it? They walk away and you're left with the same problem you had at the beginning, plus you're a bit miffed at how they treated you.

On the other hand, have you ever tried to help someone close to you with a really tough problem, like addiction or a divorce? If you know them well, respect their right to take the lead in coming up with a solution, and stick with them throughout the process, you have a pretty good chance of doing some good. But it's still difficult, and can be a long road. It would be hard to support several loved ones through these tough transitions simultaneously.

Making a real difference is about becoming a partner in the change you hope to create, instead of a pawn. Being more than a passive source of cash or free labour is your right, but it also comes with some responsibility.

In order to be a good partner, you need a pretty good understanding of the issue you're trying to impact, and you need to be prepared to stick with it for a while. That includes; being familiar with the history of the issue; understanding the perspective of the people who are affected by it; and knowing the pros and cons of common approaches to it.

This is not to say that you have to be the foremost expert on your issue before you can get involved in it. That's why you partner with professionals (like charities) who work in the cause all the time and are experts. But you do need to know enough to find professionals who are aligned with your point of view on the subject, and who you can trust.

It takes some time and commitment to first gain an understanding of your issue, develop some opinions around it, and keep up with developments in it. That's why I don't think it's reasonable to expect yourself to do that with multiple issues. It's just too much to ask, especially when giving is something that most of us do in addition to our day jobs, family commitments, and other demands on our time and attention.

If you're not prepared to make the necessary commitment but get involved anyway, you run the risk of becoming the giving equivalent of an obnoxious dinner party guest who starts issuing advice with only the most superficial understanding of any problem. Have you experienced this? You meet someone, you start talking about some concern or challenge, and before you've explained more than the basics of your situation, they've got it fixed. They know what book you must read, what person you must meet, what class you must attend, to fix the problem. They expect you to commit to doing these things. You've barely said 2 words the whole time. I don't think any of us really wants to be that person.

On the other hand, there are also people who give us advice that's very valuable. These people usually spend quite a lot of time listening and asking questions before they give any advice. They put in the effort to understand what they're talking about. In my experience, this advice has proved to be the most helpful. I'm more likely to take it, it's more likely to work, and it doesn't leave me feeling pressured or disrespected. This is the kind of do gooder we should all aspire to be.

Another reason that focusing your giving is a good idea is that it makes managing your relationships with the organizations you support easier.

In your personal life, would you rather have 50 friends you know a little and see occasionally, or 5 you know extremely well, see all the time, and could call for a 3 AM emergency?

Trying to first research, then keep in touch with, various groups working on various things can be exhausting. And it's the same for them. The more supporters a charity has, the more administration they have to do. Every donor or volunteer has to be tracked somehow. Every gift has to be thanked and receipted. Multiple supporters are a good thing if they're all involved at a significant level. In that case, the admin work is worth it for the benefit the charity receives.

But if givers are contributing minimally while requiring the same amount of work as anyone else, it can be very hard on an organization.

Concentrating support is useful, too, if we want to be heard by the organizations we support. If we have an idea or a criticism that could help the charity do a better job, but they barely know who we are, how much weight is that going to carry?

On the other hand, if we've kept in touch, demonstrated a meaningful understanding of the cause, engaged in a variety of ways, and participated in an ongoing conversation with them about the work, are they going to take us seriously? You bet they are.

And again – this level of involvement is hard to maintain if you're spread too thin. Focus is key to effectiveness, and effectiveness means actually doing good (as opposed to just saying we are). Confidence that we're actually doing good is the holy grail of the Savvy Do Gooder. So focus, my friends, even if it's tough at first.

I understand that this may sound like a lot of work. But again, this is where having a clear focus will help. It is work, yes. But will it be more of a burden than being pulled in twenty directions at once? Will it be a bigger chore than feeling like you give and give and never get anywhere with it?

Focus involves work, but it may not be more onerous than what you're already doing. You can make 20 gifts to 20 different organizations in a year, or you can make 2 gifts to 2 organizations. This frees up 18 other occasions when you would have been writing cheques and filing tax receipts. This is time you can use to read articles about your chosen issue, read the materials your 2 organizations send you, visit their locations, or call them up and find out the latest. 18 occasions' worth is probably more than you need to stay up to date – you can cut back!

The savings goes beyond just time. Once you've made the conscious decision to go narrow and deep with your giving (focusing on fewer issues and knowing them well), you will no longer have to deal with the stress of other requests. You won't have to wrestle with yourself at the supermarket counter donation box, when your coworkers put on a fundraising drive, or when those heart-tugging commercials come on the TV. When you've chosen to focus, you will feel more comfortable saying 'no' to the rest.

Plus: if you can find the right path for you, the work may actually be something you enjoy doing. You might find it rewarding and relaxing. You might enjoy reading about your issue, developing relationships with experts in the field, learning about the latest developments. It might even be fun.

Choosing the right one: what's your passion?

To narrow down the causes available to you, start by doing some soul-searching and asking,

"What's my passion?"

What is the one thing that you really, really care the most about changing? As you look at the world around you, what improvements do you just itch to make happen?

Do you see anything that drives you crazy? Some injustice or wasted opportunity that you just can't stand? Some barrier that's preventing wonderful things from happening? Some suffering that you find intolerable?

Maybe it's something that's affected you personally. Maybe you've struggled in your life, and want to make the path smoother for others. Maybe you watched a loved one go through something difficult, or even lost them, and you want to save others from the same fate.

By contrast, perhaps something amazing happened to you that's made you who you are today, and you want to extend the same opportunity to others.

These are some of the questions you can explore to narrow down the list of things you'd like to work on. This is more than a feel-good exercise. It has real practical value: Being a Savvy Do Gooder can be a lot of work. Engaging at a level where you really understand what you're doing and are making a valuable contribution takes time and energy. If you're working on something you have a passion for, you'll have the fuel in your tank to keep you going.

If you're involved in making a change that's truly meaningful to you, you won't mind putting in the time and the energy. You'll stay the course. You won't settle for anything less than what you know to be possible. A lot of the time, it might not even feel like work. It will be energizing and rewarding.

But if you get drawn into something that isn't that meaningful or relevant for you, it won't be much fun. Bumps in the road will bother you a lot more. Keeping up to date on how things are going will feel less like a pleasure and more like a chore. If things start to go off the rails, you might not have the energy to speak up about it and push through the rough patch to a solution.

There are parts of Savvy Do Gooding that aren't as sexy as the picture of giving that we're usually sold. If you've had any involvement with the charitable sector at all, you probably realize by now that it's not all just handing out soup to the homeless and delivering toys to poor kids. For that kind of front-line activity to run well, there's a whole world of infrastructure and governance behind it that has to be well built and maintained.

It might seem as if topics like impact measurement and organizational governance are super dry, and about as far away from passion as you can get. Debates about whether test scores are a good measure of the effectiveness of a school lunch program, or which software a particular charity should use to track donations can get pretty academic and technical. But the truth is, they are important things that need attention if we hope to do a good job of doing good. Passion is the only thing that makes that work tolerable, and even interesting.

Choosing the right one: where are you coming from?

Your giving is about you in more ways than one. Beyond being about what impact you want to have, it's also about what you bring to the table as a partner in that change.

Knowledge and understanding may be the most powerful reason to choose a cause based on who you are. I've sometimes heard givers say that it's selfish to give to issues that have touched us personally; that we should give to things that have nothing to do with us, so that our giving will be truly selfless.

I disagree. I believe that each of us has the best shot at impacting an issue if we have a thorough personal understanding of it. I believe that there is no giver savvier than the giver with firsthand experience of the cause.

Every issue is tremendously complex. If the problems we aim to address with our giving were easy to fix, they'd be fixed by now. If hunger really could be ended by food banks, it would be gone. If shelters were the answer to homelessness, there would be no street people anymore. Instead, their numbers grow. If digging wells and building schools in poor countries really solved global poverty, we've done enough of that that we could proclaim, "mission accomplished!" on that issue. Instead, we hear stories of schools standing empty and wells falling into disuse. It's just not that simple.

It's important that we each understand the change we're trying to make in the world. One thing that can be a big help in seeking that understanding is picking something we already know quite a bit about.

If you (or a loved one) have been a victim of something yourself, you have valuable perspective on it. Your decisions about it are likely to be much more insightful, sensitive, respectful, and ultimately, effective, than someone who's coming at it as an outsider.

If your work has brought you into contact with an issue repeatedly over a period of time, you have an understanding of how it works and what that means. You get the mechanics of what happens when it isn't dealt with well. Your decisions about it are going to be clear headed and intelligent. You're less susceptible to sentimentality and emotion around it than someone who's only been exposed to the fundraising material about it.

Far from being selfish, I think choosing a cause you understand intimately makes you a far more effective change maker. So ask yourself:

- What issues have impacted you personally in the past? Are there any affecting you now?
- What subjects do you already know quite a bit about? What knowledge and expertise do you have that could help you do good?
- Are there areas of your life where you have to deal with the effects of a problem with deeper causes (e.g. a hospital worker who treats case after case of diabetes)? Could you choose a cause that would give you the opportunity to tackle those deeper causes?

Choosing the right one: immediate need or long-term solutions?

I used to think that addressing immediate need was a poor use of charitable resources. I'll never forget the day I was stripped of that idea for good.

It was in my early days as a community fundraiser. Chatting with the head of the organization one evening after work, I was up on my soapbox, praising the value of getting at root causes of problems rather than just funding band aid solutions. Why treat the symptoms, I said, when we could cure the disease instead?

That's when my boss said to me,

"So you're ok with people dying in the streets, then?"

Oh. Huh.

No, I wasn't. And I'm still not. Her very well-made point is a good one: that people are suffering right now, and concentrating on the underlying issues that are the ultimate cause of that suffering does nothing for them today. It's not acceptable to let people suffer while we try to fix the big problems of the world. Both are important.

That being said, I personally still find working on longer-term solutions is a better fit for me. I don't find relieving immediate need as satisfying. I'm willing to tolerate the relatively drier and less tangible work of trying to solve knotty problems that cause suffering, in exchange for a chance that I might be solving something on a bigger scale.

But I know that others feel differently. These are the people who feel that if they can help just one person, their effort is worthwhile; who like to see immediate results from their giving; who can't stand to see another human being suffer. They know that someone has to feed the hungry while people like me are out there trying to end hunger; that someone has to administer chemotherapy while others are out trying to cure cancer.

We need long-term vision people, and we need immediate need people, too. But it's important to be clear about which kind of giver we are, so that we can get a sense of how successful our efforts are. Nothing frustrates me more than a poster for a food bank that says,

"End Hunger: Give to the Food Bank!"

Food banks may provide a valuable service to a lot of people, but hunger doesn't exist for lack of food banks. They do not end hunger, and if you give to one in the hopes that it will, you're not really on the right track.

So ask yourself: If there are people who find tackling root causes of issues more rewarding, and people who get more out of addressing immediate need; which one am I?

Choosing the right one: local or global?

Another important question to ask when choosing a cause is whether you should give to something that's geographically close to home, or something on the other side of the world.

There are excellent arguments for and against both. Locally, we can be closer to the work. We understand the culture and the society in which we're trying to make an impact. We might even have been affected by the issues ourselves. We have a better chance of seeing how our money is spent; it will be easier to monitor the management of our contribution. We're more likely to benefit ourselves from the good we do if we give to improve conditions in our own communities.

On the other hand, we might feel that there's less need in our communities than in other parts of the world. If we're in a position to give, it's likely that we live in places where most basic needs and rights are protected by stable governments and societies. This means that the problems that need addressing close to home are complex and difficult, whereas there are parts of the world where even simple needs go unfilled, like clean water or the right to vote.

This is the argument in favour of international giving. The cons of international giving, though, are that it's really difficult to understand the issues we're trying to impact.

I have a good friend who found herself in India a few years back as part of earning her economics degree. While she was there, the opportunity arose to participate in a monitoring project for a Canadian-funded microfinance[5] program in the city of Hyderabad.

The goal of the program was to help families in the slums reach greater financial stability. The expectation was that the women who were receiving the micro loans would use the money to start small businesses, buying things like sewing machines or the supplies for food stalls.

The reality, my friend soon found, was that they were using the money for dowries to marry their daughters well. As it happens, this is a very effective way to achieve financial stability in their world. After spending some time with these women, my friend found she couldn't disagree with their logic. Dowries were a much more culturally acceptable and much less risky route to take than entrepreneurship was.

They were also technically illegal. My friend doubted very much whether the Canadian donors she represented would be ok with playing the role of dowry provider, financial stability or no.

For her, the experience highlighted how difficult it is to try to help someone from a culture you don't share or understand. She began to believe that the value-based strings attached to the program were hampering its ability to do good.

Her story illustrates the problem with choosing an international cause over one closer to home. It's not impossible to be an effective international giver, but it's much, much more difficult. It's a much longer road to become truly and meaningfully informed about an international cause than a local one.

---

[5] Microfinance is a poverty-fighting strategy where small-scale entrepreneurs in poverty-stricken areas who don't qualify for traditional business financing are loaned very small amounts of money to enable them to grow their businesses. The theory is that in some cases, very little money is required to break the hand-to-mouth cycle these people are trapped in. Many microfinance schemes also involve the borrowers being organized into groups for accountability. The concept was pioneered by Mohammed Yunus and his Grameen Bank in Bangladesh.

With that in mind, if you still feel strongly that you'd like to focus your do gooding on international issues, don't be discouraged. Just know that it's going to mean a lot more homework to become educated and to keep up to date with the impact of your efforts.

A note on voluntourism

Voluntourism is cause-based travel: people go to areas of the world where there's need and spend some time there learning about the issues and the area. They usually perform some tasks to help out while they're there, like teaching schoolchildren or building wells and schools.

Voluntourism can be a very valuable activity, as long as it's approached properly. The key is to remember that the primary value of voluntourism is in the education it provides the voluntourist, not in the services the voluntourist provides.

Flying people thousands of miles and putting them up in accommodations that are usually better than anything the locals enjoy is not really the most efficient way to teach kids basic English, or dig a well. The money a voluntourist spends on a trip could fund far more than that person is able to provide in person, if they were to simply donate it and stay home.

But if that voluntourist makes the trek, meets the people, and gains some understanding of the issues they hope to impact with their contributions over the long run, it's worth it. Voluntourism can be a wonderful piece of an international donor's journey towards effectiveness.

Some things to watch for if you decide to be an international voluntourist:

- Make sure that you're not taking a job away from a local.
- Check the legitimacy of the organization that sets up your trip: there are many fly-by-nights and scammers who have been known to go so far as to set up fake orphanages to cheat foreign visitors out of their money.

- Try to give local people the respect and leadership they deserve in the process of addressing their own problems. Would you like it if some outsider came into your house and started 'fixing' things? Neither do they, although they may be too polite to say so.

When it comes to deciding which issue you'd like to focus your giving on, there's nothing wrong with taking your time. The old saying "haste makes waste" applies very well here.

There's nothing wrong with spending a few days, weeks, or even months on this question. Talk it over with your loved ones. Do a little reading on issues you're considering. Pay attention to your feelings: is there one that really calls to you? Is there one that fills you with hope and excitement? Is there one that fills you with indignation and the irresistible urge to do something? Those are good signs. Sit with them a bit. Explore why you feel the way you do about them.

On the other hand, are there any that make you feel guilt or shame? Are there any you feel obligated to get involved with? Have you asked yourself why?

You want to choose an issue that gives you the opportunity to create a meaningful and productive giving experience. Giving yourself the time and the permission to do a bit of homework and some soul-searching around this will set you up for success down the road.

3

Understanding human needs is half the job of meeting them.
- Adlai Stevenson

THE SECOND STEP: UNDERSTAND YOUR ISSUE

The next step is to get to know your issue. If you've chosen something with which you already have personal ties, and/or something you've been interested in for a long time, this step might go a bit quicker.

That said, it's important to have a fairly broad understanding of the issue before moving forward. If you have past involvement with your issue as a supporter, or if you've been affected by it yourself, you probably have a really deep and valuable understanding, but only from one angle.

Every cause is complex, and there are several ways of looking at it. Forging ahead without taking the time to find out about different perspectives on your issue puts you at risk. You might support an activity that only makes sense for one group of people involved. Worse, you might do something with harmful side effects.

One winter a few years back, I volunteered as a literacy tutor for an English as a Second Language (ESL) student. I thought I knew enough to be good at it. After all, language is my thing. I've been writing all my life. I'm an avid reader. I'm fascinated by other countries and other cultures. I speak three languages myself. I was sure I could help someone.

I was assigned a lovely woman from Asia who had been in Canada only a few months. If I received any training before meeting her, I don't remember it. Nevertheless, I was full of great ideas to improve my students' English skills. We would have excursions - go to the botanical gardens and name the plants, stuff like that. It was going to be great!

But my student wasn't on board. She didn't want excursions. She was sweet, but shy. She was intimidated by the idea of traipsing all over the city. She wanted to meet in the same place (a small shopping centre) every week. She wasn't open to my suggestions for different activities. All we ever did was read aloud from children's books. I became increasingly frustrated. I felt stuck. I wasn't able to observe any progress in her skills. I didn't know what to do.

Eventually, we met less and less often, then not at all. Did she learn anything? Maybe. But it wasn't nearly as much as I had hoped. Sadly, I suspect I wasted her time. I may have had some knowledge of the issue I was trying to impact, but there were huge gaps in it. I didn't understand the particular challenges of immigrant women. I didn't know anything about the experiences of others who did similar work. There may have been some best practices that would have made me a much more effective tutor. If so, I was ignorant of them. I didn't do any homework at all, and the results speak for themselves.

Mistakes happen, and we live and learn. There's no researching your way into a guarantee that your giving will produce the maximum possible good. There will always be some risk.

But that doesn't mean that a basic grounding in the issue we're trying to impact can't increase our chances of really doing good. Picking an issue you're already familiar with is a great first step. There is, however, more work to be done to really be confident that the choices you make about how to spend your time, energy and money are going to result in the results you're looking for.

The good news about this step is that if you've picked an issue that you're truly passionate about, it can be a lot of fun. A cause that means a lot to you is, by definition, something you find interesting. The process of learning more about it will be enjoyable.

As part of this step, you'll get the chance to do things like;

- Find out about events focusing on causes you're interested in
- Discover experts with fascinating new perspectives about issues you care about
- Meet new people who share your passions
- Find books and articles about things that are important to you
- See movies and television programs about subjects you find fascinating

Although I often refer to this step as 'doing homework', don't some of those sound like more fun than that? Over and above gaining a meaningful understanding of your cause, you're likely to get other benefits, like; cool new events to attend; cool new places to hang out (online and in real life); and cool new people in your life with similar passions to yours.

This is one of the ways being a Savvy Do Gooder moves giving away from being a guilt-ridden obligation, and towards being a rewarding and enjoyable experience.

Questions to explore

The goal of becoming savvy about your issue is not to become the foremost expert on the subject. No one expects you to know everything there is to know about your cause, even if that were possible. What we're hoping to accomplish with this step is enough knowledge to make intelligent choices about which organizations are a good fit for you; and which ones aren't.

Some of the questions you might want to consider as you explore your chosen cause are:

- What are the root causes and related issues?

    How did this problem become a problem? What is causing this problem? You might find out that it's deeper and more complicated than it seems at first. For example, if the cause you're trying to impact is child poverty, you might find out that the most common cause of it is something like a lack of financial literacy among low-income parents.

No cause stands alone. Disease issues are related to healthy lifestyle (prevention) issues. Domestic violence issues are related to high school graduation rates. The list goes on. In order to decide what role you, personally, want to take in being a part of the solution, it's a good idea to get an idea of the landscape your issue exists within.

- What's the history?

    When did people first identify this as a cause that needed addressing? What were the first organizations and individuals to dedicate themselves to it? Where did that happen? Did the movement spread from there? How? Why?

    Philosopher and poet George Santayana famously said,

    "Those who cannot learn from the past are doomed to repeat it."

    This is as true of giving as anything else. Why re-invent the wheel, or repeat mistakes already made? Learn the history and take advantage of the lessons of the past.

- What has and hasn't worked in the past?

    If people have been working on your issue for any length of time, different approaches have been tried. Progress has been made, and so have mistakes. There have been some major milestones and/or stumbling blocks that should be relatively easy to find out about. Again – you don't have to become the foremost expert. You're looking for the highlights and lowlights.

    Knowing this story – knowing what has contributed to past progress – is hugely valuable to your ability to pick the right partner with whom to accomplish your goals. Knowing about mistakes is just as valuable. It's important to know how the players involved dealt with those errors. Did they recover quickly? Did they make appropriate adjustments? Did they learn from the experience? Were they open and honest about the experience with their supporters and the public? The way an organization, individual, or movement handles missteps says a lot about them.

In the mid-1990s, the movement to eradicate polio suffered a setback. Anti-polio crusaders had been on an aggressive vaccination campaign for many years, with great success. Suddenly, the formerly impressive numbers showing steady decrease in polio cases started to plateau. Progress stalled.

What did the polio eradication folks do? They looked into it. They found out that a new vaccine they'd been using wasn't as effective as expected. They researched further and identified the problem. This enabled them to replace the faulty serum with a more effective version. The numbers got back on track.

Today, when speaking about their work, representatives of the movement show these numbers without shame, telling the whole story openly. When I saw a presentation on the subject recently, I was very impressed, and not just because of their impressive accomplishments in the fight against polio. I was impressed by how clear, complete and honest the information was.

If eradicating polio were my cause of choice, I would feel very confident getting involved with the organization whose presentation I saw, because I trust that they will be truthful and brave in their communications with me, and that they know how to learn from challenging situations. That goes a long way towards an organization's credibility.

- What are the different ways people are currently tackling this issue?

There's more than one way to skin a cat, and there's more than one approach to every kind of social problem imaginable.

No matter what your issue, there are probably several schools of thought about how to make the biggest dent in it. You might find one more appealing than others. There may be approaches that really turn you off.

Getting a basic idea of the different methods and philosophies around how to make the change you want to be a part of is a great step to take. Having considered this question in advance will set you up to be much better at choosing an organizational partner when and if you get to that step.

- Who are the major players in this area?

    Is there a charity that's been working on your chosen cause for far longer than anyone else? Is there a newer one taking groundbreaking and revolutionary steps?

    Are there recognized experts on the subject? Do they have websites, write blogs, publish books, or give speeches?

    These are valuable resources both for getting educated initially, and for keeping up with cause-related news and trends on an ongoing basis. Chances are, there are people out there devoting their lives to knowing everything there is to know about your cause. If you find out who they are and follow the work of the ones who resonate with you, they will act as a filter and serve up relevant info on a silver platter. This is truer than ever in the age of social media.

    Depending on your issue, this may be a good time to find out who the players are near where you live. Maybe there's a world renowned expert teaching at the local college. Maybe there's a meet-up group gathering to discuss the cause.

Here are just a few of the ways you might find the information you're looking for to answer the kinds of questions above. There are many more.

Where to get the lowdown

Everyone has their own personal preferences for learning. There's no right or wrong way to get the knowledge and understanding you need to make savvy decisions about making a difference. Choose the one(s) that works for you. The most important criteria for a knowledge-gathering method is that it be something you will actually do. If you're not much of a reader, for example, don't expect yourself to get through multiple heavy books and articles about your topic.

Here are a few of the strategies you might want to consider to get savvy about your issue. It's probably a good idea to use at least 2 types of information sources, to make sure your perspective is well-rounded. Use the combination that works best for you:

- Books and articles:
  If it exists, there's probably a book about it. If you're a reader, the bookstore and the library are your best friends at this stage of the process. You can find incredible amounts of literature on just about every topic under the sun. The biggest challenge is probably going to be narrowing down the list of reading options to the ones that will be most useful and relevant to you. If you've chosen a subject you already have some knowledge about, this will be a bit easier. Another option to consider is reading scholarly articles, which tend to be shorter and more specific. If there's a university or college near where you live, they are likely to have online databases of articles searchable by keyword. An afternoon spent poking around one of those databases could yield a lot of valuable insight.

- Documentaries:
  Documentary films can be a great way to gain perspective on an issue. A good documentary can be entertaining, moving, and educational. Many towns and cities have documentary film series or festivals, and the public library can be a great resource for them as well. The availability of documentaries online is also growing all the time through on demand services and online streaming video sites.

- Events:
  There may be a conference about the issue you're interested in that you can attend. There may be a monthly social for people who care about it. It's possible that there's a speaker series in your town. There might be online webinars available. If you're a social person, events can be a fantastic way to connect with and learn from

others working on the cause you've chosen to impact. Meetup.com is just one of the ways you can find these events.

- Blogs:
There is now a free service called Google Blogs where you can search for blogs by keyword. This is a great way to get started finding online web logs about the things you're interested in. Once you find a few bloggers whose work you enjoy, chances are they will lead you to more. Bloggers routinely link to one another and post on each others' sites. Blogs are great because the good ones are updated frequently, so they offer the latest information and analysis.

If you're fairly comfortable in the online world, blogs are a great way to get informed and stay informed.

- Professionals:
Sometimes when I'm looking for info, I simply want to ask someone who would know. If you're
like me, why not seek out a pro?

Chances are, someone is making a living working on the issue you're interested in. Non-profit staff, academics, and even business people might be among the individuals on the front lines of the work you care about. If you want to save street kids, the perspective of a public defender could be extremely enlightening. If you want to fight crime, a police officer might give you a lot of food for thought. If you want to help people with mental health issues, a counselor at a drop in centre could be very informative.

Having a conversation with one of the people who live your issue every day can be a very interesting and valuable experience.

A word of caution about professionals: it's important to be clear with them that you're in the information-gathering stage. Especially when it comes to charities, many of the people whose jobs it is to talk to members of the public are also responsible for recruiting supporters. They might assume your inquiries are the first step in your becoming a donor or a volunteer, and try to push you down that road. It's not time for that yet – be clear that you're not ready to talk about involvement at this stage.

- Podcasts:

    Do you spend a fair amount of time plugged in to your earphones, or in your car? Maybe the best way for you to get the info you need is via audio. There are lots of podcasts available (not to mention audio books) that can provide a ton of great info about a variety of subjects.

- The World Wide Web:

    I could probably write a whole book about all the different ways to get info from the internet, besides the ones already mentioned here. From joining a Facebook group to participating in webinars to just plain Googling your subject, the possibilities are endless. If you're already the kind of person who likes getting their info online, you probably don't need me to tell you how. Go forth and discover!

The surprise you might be in for

In the process of learning about your cause, you may discover something unexpected and a bit challenging:

As you read/discuss/watch information about how people have made an impact in the past, and about the most promising strategies for making more in the future, you might discover that those methods don't involve charities.

It's entirely possible that the best way to impact your issue is not by giving to charity. You might find out that the biggest advances in your area haven't come about as a result of philanthropy or volunteerism at all.

When you think about it, it's really quite odd that we're in the habit of always associating social good with the charitable sector; that we have a dividing line between charities and the rest of human endeavour. It's not like charities are the only ones that ever do anything good or make a difference. Nor is it true that everything charities do leads to positive change in the world.

So it's perfectly reasonable that as we learn more about how to make change happen, we might find out that the most logical path doesn't include formal charities, or that it involves them only in a supporting role.

Consider the issue of disaster relief, for example. In a 2 year period, both Haiti and Japan suffered large-scale disasters related to earthquakes. Haiti's earthquake was less severe on the Richter scale than Japan's. Japan's population density was much higher than Haiti's. Japan's crisis was amped up by a tsunami and by the threat of nuclear meltdown at power plants in the affected area. Haiti did not experience those complicating factors.

So which country suffered the most loss of life? Haiti did. By a landslide. Ten times more people died in the Haiti earthquake than in the Japanese multi-disaster.[6]

Was it because Japan had more charities on the ground when the quake hit, ready to respond? Far from it. As an ongoing humanitarian quagmire, Haiti had any number of non-governmental organizations (NGOs) well-entrenched in their territory long before the ground started shaking. By comparison, Japan had only a couple of international organizations on site, plus the usual mix of domestic charities typical of a prosperous country.

Was it because the international relief charities responded more enthusiastically for Japan than for Haiti? Hardly. Within days of the Haitian crisis, international NGOs descended on the island nation in droves. The same cannot be said of their response to the Japanese disaster, although it wasn't for lack of trying. In the immediate aftermath of the event, Japanese authorities were very clear that they didn't want outside help, except in very specific ways that they would manage themselves. As it turned

---

[6] Earth: The Science Behind the Headlines. *Voices: From Haiti to Japan: A Tale of Two Disaster Recoveries.* March 9, 2012.
http://www.earthmagazine.org/article/voices-haiti-japan-tale-two-disaster-recoveries [July 31, 2012]

out, this consisted mainly of direct requests to other governments for specialized search and rescue teams and supplies. One European charitable organization went so far as to show up at a Japanese airport, only to be sent packing immediately.

Two years on from the Haitian quake, stories are starting to come out about mismanagement of funds. Questions are being asked about why the island's still in a state of chaos. Most of the development and relief charities are still on the scene. The compound where many of them are based has been mocked for being more luxurious than the places most of the citizens are living in. Meanwhile, Japan seems to be recovering nicely.

So for someone who's decided that disaster relief is the issue they really want to tackle, what's the lesson here? What real impact did charity have in these two cases? Some of the organizations probably did some good but on balance, the disaster with the most charitable involvement had a far more catastrophic fallout.

What were the elements that actually made a difference? How did Japan weather their storm so well?

These questions are always debatable, of course, and I'm no disaster expert. But it appears that the main factor that saved the Japanese people from Haiti's fate was preparedness. Their people were well-educated about what to do in case of an emergency. Their country had all the right infrastructure for things like early warnings, efficient evacuation, and coordinated recovery. They were ready.

In my view, this boils down to the government and the culture. As a country, Japan recognized the threat their geological position put them in and took the appropriate steps to make ready. Public investment was made. Systems were kept up to date. Every citizen was made aware of the danger and given the tools to deal with it. When the worst case scenario came true, the state was strong enough to maintain control and manage the response. They had good relationships and communications channels within the international community, enabling them to reach out for help in a controlled and appropriate way.

Haiti, meanwhile, hasn't had a strong and stable government since colonial times. They barely have roads, never mind sophisticated communications channels. Their people are lucky if they learn to read, never mind how to deal with crumbling buildings. Haiti is notorious in the international community for being, well, a mess. The damage they suffered was a foregone conclusion before the first tremor hit, and there was little the charities could do except mop up afterwards.

So if you're a person who feels strongly about reducing the suffering caused by natural disasters, is your best bet to contribute to relief charities? Maybe.

Maybe you feel that there will always be disasters in unstable parts of the world, and someone has to go in and provide basic relief for those affected. In that case, charity could be the right path for you. If you've decided that addressing immediate needs feels right to you, you might find that route very rewarding.

But if you decide that it doesn't fit your vision, if you'd rather prevent the suffering in the first place, then charity may not be the way to go. You may want to get more involved with government. You may want to take a look at the disaster preparedness situation of your own area. That might lead you, for instance, to get to know the folks in charge of preparedness in your own backyard, and find out how you can support them.

Maybe you can have the biggest impact by informing your elected officials that preparedness is a priority for you. Maybe the best strategy is to get in touch with the local school board and make them aware of the importance of educating the children about what to do in case of emergencies.

Perhaps your passion lies at the international level, so the best approach is to reach out to high-level government officials who play on the global scene, lobbying them to work towards greater international cooperation with other countries around disaster issues. Maybe you find out how you can contribute to the development of governments in disaster-prone areas.

Or maybe you could do what my father did. He worked in the military, then for the provincial government for many years. He learned a lot, and he saw the fallout from disasters for individuals and industry. There were government regulations and requirements around preparedness, at least for industry. There was, however, something missing. There was little help available to meet those requirements. People were being told what goals to hit, but had no clear blueprint for how to do it.

Existing certifications and educational programs were, in his opinion, inadequate. He was seeing damage from tornadoes, floods, and chemical releases that he knew was preventable. Although government fines were levied and disaster relief was paid out, it couldn't undo the damage. Nor did it prevent the same mistakes from happening each time an emergency or disaster struck. My father became increasingly frustrated.

So he did a very brave thing. Even though he had a young family to support, he quit his safe government job. He set up shop in the basement of our small rented house in Edmonton and started offering consulting services to anyone who wanted to limit their losses, prevent suffering, and comply with regulations.

Because of those regulations, there was a healthy market for this service. With a lot of hard work and the steadfast support of my mother, he was able to build a successful business and eventually turn a profit. But he could have done that any number of ways. He chose to do it in a way that also made a difference in area that's important to him. He sincerely cared about limiting the damage done by disasters.

Twenty years later, he has a staff of 8. Together as Emergency Response Management Consulting, they've helped people all over the world improve their disaster preparedness. From Malaysia to Columbia to Canada, people are ready for the worst thanks to this 'little business that could'. Wanting to have an even greater impact, they also took over the management of Disaster Forum, one of the premier crisis management conferences in the country. Every year, about 300 professionals gather in Banff, Alberta, to learn about their field and make connections with others doing the same.

My dad has made all of this happen without any involvement from a registered charitable organization of any kind. Yet few could argue that his work hasn't had a positive impact.

This is an excellent example of how business, too, can be a force for good.

So as you learn and explore in your chosen issue area, keep an open mind. Don't limit yourself to charity-related tactics. If your research is leading you towards some other method for making a difference, go with that! You might find yourself in exciting new territory, and the road might lead to you doing more good than you ever could following the traditional channels.

Remember that you don't have to come out of this step with a fully-formed and rigid theory of change for your issue. The idea is to get a good sense of what's going on in the area, but leave enough flexibility that when you begin talking to organizations you might support, you're open to hearing their ideas and strategies.

If you've done that, and you still believe you'd like to include giving to charity in your path to making a difference, you're ready to move on to the next step and choose your partners.

4

*Follow your heart,
but take your brain with you.*

- Anonymous

THE THIRD STEP: PICK THE RIGHT PARTNER

Sometimes, dealing with a charity can feel like a transaction: they ask, you give, they thank you. Rinse and repeat. Your role is to pony up the cash. You're the ATM of the situation.

Although this is quite common, it isn't the best way for things to work; neither for the charities nor for the givers. Ideally, it should work more like a partnership; a relationship. People are more than a passive resource-dispensing machine. You're not an ATM. You have a lot to offer beyond handing over whatever money or time is requested.

Giving to charity is a relationship

Giving to charity should be a two-way street: You and the charity have shared goals, and each of you has a particular role in creating the change you want to see; they have expectations of you and you have expectations of them; good communication is vital. Just like in any other relationship.

And just like any other relationship, it's not going to work with just anyone. Some people work well together and some people don't. That doesn't mean that people who don't work well together are bad people – it's just important to find the right fit.

The same is true of finding the right charitable organization to team up with. People often ask me which charities are the 'best' ones, and I can never give them a simple answer. I firmly believe that there is no 'best' charity – but there is a best charity for you.

Often, the word "charity" is treated as if it means the same thing as "good", automatically, and for everyone. The phrase "giving to charity" is treated as synonymous with "doing good", no matter what charity we're talking about. But all charities have different missions, and different approaches. As the mass sterilization example in chapter 2 illustrates, for every issue or problem, there are dozens of different ways to tackle it, and you may not be on board with all of them.

Even if an organization has chosen an approach to change that you agree with, they still might not be the right partner for you. They might be poorly managed, or they might mistreat their staff. You may not agree with the way they handle their finances. You might not like the way they fundraise. Perhaps they take too many risks for your taste, or too few. The list goes on.

Finding the right fit: whose job is it?

Although the relationship between a charity and its supporters should be a two-way street, who do you think the burden of finding the right fit falls on? I'll give you a hint: I've rarely heard of a charity turning down prospective donors.

That's right, friends: it's on us, the would-be do gooders. I often think of this when I read about a charity that's had its charitable status revoked. The headlines scream "FRAUD!", "CHARITY SCAM EXPOSED!", "DONORS OUTRAGED!", and take a very sympathetic position toward the poor, hoodwinked givers.

When charity goes bad: where does the buck stop?

There are probably a few cases where the charity staff deliberately mislead the donors, who cannot know what they are getting themselves into. It's hard to say where real dishonesty is at play, as opposed to incompetence or some other less malicious factor.

Often, though, these 'poor, innocent victims' of charity fraud never ask any meaningful questions about the organizations they invest in before forking over their funds. In a recent study, Hope Consulting found that fewer than 30% of people ask any questions at all before giving to charity[7]. No wonder fly-by-night, mismanaged, and fraudulent charities manage to get funded.

Take the One Million Shirts scandal, for example. In 2010, an internet marketer called Jason Sadler decided to collect a million t-shirts and send them to the poor in Africa. He managed to collect a lot of shirts and a lot of money for shipping, but before long, he also collected a boatload of hate from the aid community.

You see, according to the experts, Africans are not in need of free shirts, or free shoes, or any other castoffs from the west. The aid workers argued that these kinds of 'donations' have multiple negative effects on the development of the very areas they're meant to help; the flood of free stuff depresses local markets and takes jobs away from locals; the underlying assumption that Africans need and want whatever we in the west decide to send them is patronizing and insulting; the money spent to haul all that free stuff across the ocean could be better spent on other things.

The point is this: what were Mr. Sadler's donors thinking? What made them believe that a young man whose background is in t-shirt advertising and who had never even been to Africa was the right person to lead a foreign aid project? The idea is pretty preposterous. Maybe Mr. Sadler was misguided, but he would never have gotten anywhere with his bad idea if no one had supported him.

An example closer to home came up as part of the response to the 2011 forest fires that wiped out a third of the town of Slave Lake in my home province of Alberta, Canada. A company in a nearby city decided to take up a collection of used goods in cardboard boxes for the victims of the tragedy. When they tried

---

[7] Hope Consulting, *Money for Good: The US Market for Impact Investments and Charitable Gifts from Individual Donors and Investors* May 2010 http://hopeconsulting.us/pdf/Money%20for%20Good_Final.pdf [July 31, 2012]

to send their boxes to Slave Lake, however, they were turned down. Apparently, Slave Lake already had all the hand-me-downs they could use.

The company then tried to give their boxes to various charities in their area, with no success. No one could use the stuff they had collected. Finally, it ended up with a for-profit outfit that claimed it would find a home for it. Shortly thereafter, some of the boxes were discovered at the dump. People were outraged – it made the news. Angry commentators accused the charities who turned the stuff down of being a bunch of scammers; frauds who don't appreciate what they're given. Everyone felt awful for the kind hearted donors who'd had their contributions wasted.

But here's the thing – no one needed this stuff. The employees at the company where the stuff was collected did not bother to find out whether what they were doing was needed before they did it. They may have had good intentions, but the fact that the experts (charities and Slave Lake town officials) didn't buy in to their poorly-thought-through project does not make them hard done by.

Have you ever known someone who's constantly in crisis mode? Always getting taken advantage of by someone or other? They date jerks, con artists, and abusers. They let their relatives walk all over them. They're overworked and underappreciated in their jobs. No matter how many times they change partners or jobs, it's always the same story.

Don't you eventually run out of sympathy for these people? Start to wonder what it is about them that keeps getting them into these situations? Wish they would change whatever it is that keeps attracting the wrong kind of attention?

That's kind of how I feel about the public and charity scams. If people put no effort into vetting the organizations they support, it's not surprising that they get burned.

Each one of us has the power to prevent this – we can take a savvier approach, do our homework, and pick the right partner. This will go a long way towards keeping us safe from scammers and blunderers. Because you're reading this book, I know you're ready to choose this savvier, safer road.

That's great – now, you'll need some tools.

Evaluating charities

There are several charity evaluators out there, gathering and analyzing all kinds of information about charities. Each of them has a different approach, and each of them offers valuable information about both organizations and issues.

All of them are, in my opinion, slightly flawed, and all for the same reason: they're all looking for a way to rate and/or rank charities based on some objective standard of worthiness. This is, I think, an impossible task.

Charities do everything from cleaning up oil spills to offering grief counseling. I simply don't think it's possible to find one yardstick capable of sizing them all up. Again, there is no 'best' charity – it's a question of finding the right one for you.

So although these evaluators offer a lot of data and analysis that can be very helpful in the process of choosing an organization to get involved with, I recommend you take their 'scores' and 'recommendations' with a grain of salt.

For example: GiveWell (givewell.org) is one of the most prominent charity evaluators around. They have a very elaborate and well-thought out process for analyzing various organizations. But – all their reasoning is based on the basic assumption that it's better to give overseas than locally. You may agree with that, and be totally comfortable with GiveWell's recommendations. But if you happen to believe that giving locally is better, their advice will be less useful for you, personally.

Some of the other well-known evaluators that you might find useful are:

- Charity Navigator (charitynavigator.org)
- Guidestar (guidestar.org)
- Charity Intelligence Canada (charityintelligence.ca)
- Place2Give (place2give.com)

- Better Business Bureau Wise Giving Alliance (bbb.org/us/charity)
- GreatNonProfits (greatnonprofits.org)
- Charity Focus (charityfocus.ca)

The best charity evaluation tool I've ever seen

In contrast to the raters and the rankers, there is a charity evaluation tool that I think is absolutely fantastic. It's something that anyone can use to sort out which organization is going to work best for them; and it's straightforward and simple.

I believe that by using this tool, you can put yourself in an excellent position to make an informed choice about who to partner with.

What is this miracle tool, you ask? It's called the Charting Impact 5 Questions[8]. It was developed by the Better Business Bureau Wise Giving Alliance, GuideStar USA, and IndependentSector.org to help nonprofit organizations improve the quality of their reporting to supporters, but I think it works just as well as a tool for supporters to use in evaluating organizations.

The key difference between the 5 Questions and every other evaluation tool I've seen is that it's less like a standardized test and more like a job interview. The questions are targeted and meaningful, but they don't produce a score. They frame a conversation between you and a charity about the things that matter.

Here are the 5 Questions as they appear on the Charting Impact website, with my own version of the commentary. The original wording was intended for non-profits to use when writing reports about their work:

1. What is the organization aiming to accomplish?

---

[8] Charting Impact http://www.chartingimpact.org/about/ [July 31, 2012]

What is the organization's ultimate goal for intended impact? Identify the groups or communities they aim to assist, the needs their work is addressing, and the expected outcomes. Examine how their goals for the next three to five years (or an alternate timeframe specified in your answer) fit within their overall plan to contribute to lasting, meaningful change.

Why is this answer important?

Articulating the organization's long-term goals helps us understand their mission and intended outcomes. It also gives context and purpose to their day-to-day activities. The response to this question is the foundation for the responses to the other four. Even if you are an immediate-needs oriented giver, it's a very good idea to get a sense of the bigger picture right from the start.

2. What are their strategies for making this happen?

   What are the organization's strategies for accomplishing the long-term goals cited in the previous answer? Ask them to specify the broad approaches they employ, and why they believe these methods will benefit the target audience or advance the issue. Ask them to lay out near-term activities that serve as important building blocks for future success, explaining how these elements strengthen the organization's strategic approach.

   Why is this answer important?

   Clearly articulated strategies help those of us outside the organization understand how they aim to accomplish their long-term goals. The long-term strategic approach also helps determine appropriate near-term activities.

3. What are the organization's capabilities for doing this?

   Ask them to detail the resources, capacities, and connections that support their progress towards long-term goals. While describing their organization's core assets, they should identify both internal resources (including, but not limited to, staff, budget, and expertise) and external strengths (including partnerships, networks, and influence) that have contributed to, or will contribute in the future to, the accomplishment of these goals. Also ask about any future resources and tools that will further strengthen your work.

Why is this answer important?

Identifying the organization's specific capabilities and how they are aligned with their long-term goals can give you confidence that these resources are being utilized constructively. The purpose is not to get a list of every resource, but to identify how the organization's capabilities, both internal and external, will contribute to your intended impact.

4. How will the organization know if it's making progress?

What are the key qualitative and quantitative indicators against which the organization assesses progress toward their intended impact? In addition to describing what they measure, ask them to identify key milestones – what their interim targets are, and when they want to reach them – that signal progress and success. Ask for a description of their assessment and improvement process: the qualitative and quantitative methods they use as they monitor key indicators, and how the organization uses and will use that information to refine their efforts.

Why is this answer important?

By definition, a long-term goal is not accomplished overnight. Monitoring key indicators and marking important accomplishments along the way help an organization stay on track, instill confidence in its methods, and let both internal and external stakeholders track movement toward achieving long-term goals. If you are a more immediate-needs focused giver, you may want to look at this question in a slightly different way. You may want to ask how the organization knows that, overall, it's doing more good than harm.

I'll never forget the Christmas Eve when I met a homeless woman asking for enough money to get a cheap hotel room for the night. When I asked her why she didn't just go to the

69

shelter (2 blocks away), she explained that she'd been clean for months, but if she went there, she would be surrounded by drugs and users. It would be very hard for her not to relapse. So what seemed like the perfect answer to her immediate needs was, in fact, a great danger. Sometimes, even knowing how much good is being done through immediate-needs work can be trickier than it seems.

5. What have and haven't they accomplished so far?

Can they demonstrate recent progress toward long-term goals by describing how the near-term objectives are propelling the organization toward their ultimate intended impact? Go beyond the outputs of the work to find out how these outcomes are contributing to fulfilling long-term goals. In discussing both outcomes achieved and those not yet realized, include what the organization has learned about what does and doesn't work, what risks and obstacles exist, and what adjustments to goals, strategies, or objectives have been made along the way.

Why is this answer important?

Sharing the outcomes of recent work offers an opportunity to reflect on the organization's purpose, while affirming that progress that has been made toward long-term goals. Focusing on outcomes—and not just outputs—also improves an organization's ability to identify important strategies and variables affecting pursuit of the ultimate impact.

With the 5 Questions in hand, you're ready to start investigating charities in earnest. You might be able to answer all 5 without a personal interview – if a charity's website and promotional materials are really good, they might contain all the info you need.

More likely, though, you'll want to have a live conversation with a representative of the charity you're considering. If possible, it's a good idea to visit them in person. Depending on the kind of work they do, you might be able to take a tour of their facilities and/or meet some of the people their work is affecting.[9] Even if the charity's work is mostly done in an office, it can be good to visit and get a sense of how the place is run, what the people who work there are like, etc.

Again, there are no 'right' or 'wrong' charities. The purpose of evaluating a charity you're thinking of giving to is to find one you're comfortable with, one you can trust. There are no 'correct' answers to the 5 Questions, but when you ask them, you'll know whether or not you feel right about the answers you get.

Since you've done your homework on the charity's issue, and particularly if you have some pre-existing connection to it, you'll know when you've found a good fit, or a red flag.

The final piece: how will the organization treat you?

Sometimes, we may forgive a charity for treating us in a way we don't like if we believe they are doing good work:

- Maybe they sent you five appeals in response to your one gift? That's ok – they're doing good work.

- Maybe they botched the production of your tax receipt? That's ok – they mean well.

- Maybe they failed to let you know about the results of your contribution? That's ok – they're busy focusing on the important part of the work.

This is another area where you need to know what you need out of the relationship, and make sure you get it. Maybe you don't mind a little disorganization. Maybe multiple requests for

---

[9] Be careful with this one – charity recipients often feel obligated to meet donors, even if it makes them uncomfortable. Try to keep this in mind – few people are proud to be accepting charity, and it's important to treat the people you're trying to help with respect. They might agree to meet you, but that doesn't mean it's a good idea. Consider having a frank discussion with the charity representative about this before going ahead with plans to meet beneficiaries.

support don't bother you. Maybe you're ok with having to ask for results info.

Or maybe you absolutely don't want to be asked for money more than once a year. Maybe you want regular updates on the work you're helping to pay for. Maybe you expect a high level of administrative management.

Do you prefer to be contacted by mail, phone, or email? Do you want to be invited to fundraising events? If you volunteer, do you need a lot of direction, or are you ok with being left to figure things out for yourself?

It's important to make sure the relationship works for you, so it makes sense to find out how a charity treats its supporters before becoming one. The alternative is to find out the hard way – through disappointment and frustration. Asking the charity about their supporter relations is one way to cover this, but it's also a good idea to ask for references – maybe even meet with someone who's already involved with the organization, and ask them about the things that matter to you.

Again, it's not really a question of the charity being bad or good. It's about whether or not you're going to have a good experience supporting them.

By using the information available through the various charity evaluators out there, doing your own reconnaissance using the 5 Questions, and finding out whether their supporter relations approach is going to work for you, you'll have everything you need to pick the right partner to make the change you want to see in the world.

5

Our societies have trained us to give and accept help when, in fact, what is needed is full engagement, collaboration and partnership.

- Lynne Twist

THE FOURTH STEP: BUILD YOUR RELATIONSHIPS

When you pick the charity you want to give to, you've started a partnership, but it's only the beginning. It's like you've been on your first date and you've agreed to hang out again, but the best is (hopefully) yet to come.

Especially when it comes to donating money, once the cash is handed over, a lot of people treat the process as basically over. Sure, there'll probably be a thank-you letter of some kind, and a tax receipt at some point, but that's about it.

When you think about it, that's kind of weird. It's like wanting to buy an item, figuring out where it's sold, walking in to the store and telling them what you want, having them say, "We have that – it costs XX dollars", giving them the money, being thanked, and leaving.

See what's missing? You never got what you paid for. You didn't stick around long enough to find out if they delivered.

It's not a perfect metaphor, but it does highlight the pure silliness of checking out of the charity relationship after giving your money or participating in an event. To really create change, giving cannot be treated as a transaction that happens once and is over. It's ongoing – it's a relationship.

As a relationship, it takes a certain amount of work, but it can yield significant benefits if that work is done. By keeping in touch with the charity(ies) you give to, you get to find out what your giving is accomplishing. You deepen your understanding of the issue you care so much about. And you set yourself up to be much more than a one-time volunteer or cash donor.

The power of YOU

You have something to give that goes far beyond time or money. The charity sees its operations from a certain perspective – especially when it comes to donors and volunteers. You, on the other hand, represent the other side of the equation. You know how it feels to be on the receiving end of their communications, appeals, advertising, volunteer management, etc.

You are their market. Most charities don't have the resources to conduct market research – surveys, focus groups, etc. You'd be surprised how oblivious they can be about how their actions come across to the people they rely on for support. As an involved and informed member of that group, you have the ability to fill them in. You have the credibility to express that point of view and be taken seriously.

This is not about picking on them or tearing them down. Never forget that the ultimate goal is to help the charity do things better. If they operate better, more good will get done, and isn't that why we're all in this for?

By genuinely wanting to help, and always being respectful and productive in your approach, you can be an incredibly valuable resource to your chosen charity partner.

If they choose not to use your feedback, that's ok, it's all part of the relationship. They're under no obligation to do as you suggest, and of course, they may have information that you don't. But they should at least be prepared to listen, consider your input, and let you know what they decide to do about it.

Understand the roles

Charities do exist to carry out the change that you want to see in the world, and they do need your contributions to do it. In a way, that makes you their boss. But there's something very important to remember about that.

The people working for charities are professionals. If you've chosen a good quality, well run charity, it will be staffed by people who've devoted their lives to their cause. No one goes into charity work for the money. Many of them will have studied the issue for years, and/or have front line experience working on it.

Charity professionals know a lot that you don't. Like you, they bring something to the relationship that has to be recognized and respected. Just because you're putting in the money or volunteer labour, it doesn't mean that you know better than them how to go about things.

I've seen too many situations where charity professionals bend over backwards trying to fit into their donors' idea of how they should do things, even if they know there's a better way. No donors means no money, and money makes the charity world go 'round, so the donor's always right, right? It's tragic to see the wasted opportunities this creates sometimes.

I encourage you to not be the kind of giver who expects to be treated as 'always right'. Respect the knowledge and experience that the professionals bring to the situation. At its best, giving is a true partnership, with each party valuing and respecting the contributions of the other.

Keeping current

What does 'maintaining the relationship' look like after the giving is done, the tax receipt is issued, and the thank-you letter is filed away? There are lots of different ways to keep in touch with your organization(s) of choice.

As fitness experts say about exercising, "The best form of exercise is the one you'll do." This is also true of keeping up with your organization(s). Here are some options:

- Keep in touch with a human being: Depending on the charity you're involved with, you may have the opportunity to meet in person with a representative of the organization. Visit them at their office, take them for coffee, or lunch every once in a while. Have a chat. Ask about how the programs are going. Ask about whatever you're curious about. Be careful not to overstep with this – charity staff are often stretched thin, and their time is valuable. Make sure you're respectful of their time and other commitments.
- Volunteer: To keep tabs on the organization, be a part of the organization. It can be a great way to get insight about how things are run. Depending on your circumstances and the organization, you could do anything from sitting on a board making big decisions about how the charity is run, to serving soup at a homeless shelter.
- Read what they send you: Most good charities have reporting in place to let their donors know what's happening with their contributions. Often, they will send paper copy to your home, or issue an electronic newsletter.
- Connect via social media: More and more organizations of all kinds are getting into the world of virtual networks – take advantage of it! Follow your organization on Twitter, like them on Facebook, etc. The great thing about social media is that it's not one-way communication. It gives you an opportunity to comment and question, participating in conversations with the organization and with other supporters.

How much or how little time you spend on this is up to you – I recommend taking a long, hard look at what you're invested in at least once a year. If you prefer to save up all the materials and dig into them annually before deciding to renew or discontinue your support, that works.

Or if you like to stay connected on an ongoing basis, that's great, too. As long as you're deliberately reviewing your support regularly, rewarding the organization for continuing to do good work, or withdrawing your support if your requirements aren't being met.

Consider periodically going back to the 5 Questions from Chapter 4. Ask them again, and see how your charity is doing against your expectations.

Giving should always be based on performance. If an organization is consistently not delivering on their promises, make sure you're aware of it so you can quit while you're ahead.

Look out for Number One

In 2011, Meryl Streep played Margaret Thatcher in The Iron Lady - a role for which she won a well-deserved Oscar.

The life of this iconic figure (Thatcher, not Streep) brings up an interesting point about charity. For her, ambition always came first. She felt she had a duty to do something with her life beyond marriage and motherhood, and she made her choices accordingly. She expected her family to understand. She had important work to do, and seemed to take it for granted that they would quietly take a back seat and act as a support system.

The parallel with charity is that sometimes, charitable organizations act like Thatcher. They have important causes to champion, vital work to do. They need support and resources - from people like us. Their donors, their volunteers.

But do they sometimes treat us as Thatcher appears to have treated her family - expecting us to put up with a certain amount of neglect and bad treatment in the interest of the greater good?

When charities respond to gifts with requests for more, bombard supporters with highly emotional and urgent requests, fail to give meaningful feedback about what our giving is accomplishing, or don't consider how we'd like to be treated - is that the equivalent of Margaret Thatcher's expectation that her family be by her side for photo shoots and speeches, and selflessly keep the home fires burning while she was out crusading for what she believed in?

I believe it is, and I believe that while it may have worked for the Thatchers, in the long run it does not work for charities and their supporters.

Pursuing a good cause does not give an organization the right to treat you, its supporter, badly. In the big picture, that's just going to wear you out, turn you off, and reduce the support the charity gets. It's bad business, and it should be discouraged.

The fundraising factor

This is never more true than in the case of fundraising. It's amazing to me how common it is for intelligent people to think that it's ok to be pushy, inappropriate, and emotionally manipulative in the name of raising money for a good cause.

The most painful example of this that I've seen appeared in the blog of someone I normally admire very much – bestselling author Seth Godin.

I read Seth's blog every day. Usually, it's full of amazing insights about marketing, tribes, and respect; very thought provoking. He wrote a post in the summer of 2011, though, that was different. It was entitled The Buzzing in my Ear Didn't Mean I Was About to Die. Basically, it's a fundraising appeal. Seth is part of the creation of a book, the revenue of which will go to an anti-malaria charity.

The post starts with a nightmare scenario, asking readers to imagine not being able to afford needed malaria medication for their kids. Then it gives 3 commands; things we must do "right this minute, right now". The first is to buy the book, the other two involve promoting the book to friends.

He goes on to explain that it will fund bed nets for malaria-prone areas. That may or may not be the best use of charitable dollars, but that's not what really bothered me.

I revere Seth Godin for his extraordinary insights about respect in marketing. One of his biggest books is Permission Marketing, in which he advocates against 'interruption marketing'. Don't ambush people. Don't be pushy. Make it about them, not you.

Make it about what they care about, their problems. Offer them something they truly need.

I could be reading him wrong, but I'm pretty sure these are fundamental tenets of 'Seth Godin the marketing guru'.

As I see it, 'Seth Godin the fundraiser' is in violation of those tenets. Going to a blog I read for marketing info and being told I must immediately buy a book to end malaria does not feel respectful. It feels like being ambushed.

Being made to feel guilty because I don't have children who need malaria medication does not feel respectful. It feels invasive.

Being told I have to involve myself RIGHT NOW in something I know little about, or lives will be lost, certainly doesn't feel respectful. It feels pushy.

What does Seth know about my needs as a charitable giver? Nothing. The fact that I subscribe to his blog tells him I have an interest in the things he specializes in, not in ending malaria. I gave him permission to give me orders about marketing, not about ending malaria.

I trust him as an expert, but not on this subject. If he urged me to go out and buy a certain book about marketing RIGHT NOW, I would take that seriously, because that's the area where he's earned my trust.

Why is there a different rule book for charity?

Why is it that even the most enlightened of thinkers bend the rules when it comes to fundraising? Why are things that would normally be unacceptable suddenly ok if they're 'for a good cause'?

Why do we assume that off-putting behaviour will not have consequences as long as our intentions are pure?

This is not to say that Seth should never use his blog to talk about causes he feels passionately about, but there is a respectful way to do that. He could share why he cares, why he chooses to support particular organizations or initiatives, post links to them, encourage readers to check it out and make their own decisions. He did do some of this, but then blew it by putting the pressure on.

He is well positioned to connect readers to malaria experts and give those experts the opportunity to earn their trust and support. That would be a positive thing. It would be a respectful invitation to engage.

If something a charity you're involved with does to solicit support rubs you the wrong way, don't be afraid to speak up about it. This is especially true if they're asking you to do things that don't feel right, like pressuring your friends for support, or going door-to-door asking for contributions.

Express your concerns and, if it you don't feel that they're addressed, consider voting with your feet. It's important that the giving community sends a clear message to fundraisers (even volunteer ones) that the fundraising that makes people feel pressured, uncomfortable, and guilty is not acceptable.

If we can do that, we will all be better off, and conversations about support can focus on more meaningful and rewarding topics – like what positive change looks like, and how to create it.

Conclusion

At this point, do you find yourself a bit overwhelmed? Thinking that perhaps the Savvy Do Gooder version of giving is too much for you to take on?

Does the process of soul searching, followed by issue research, followed by organization research, then giving, and finally, keeping in the loop afterwards, all sound a bit daunting?

That's certainly understandable, but consider this: you can spend as much or as little time on each of these steps as you like. I've tried to give you plenty of food for thought on each one, but that doesn't mean they have to be long and painful.

Quickie Savvy Do Gooding

Imagine you hear about a humanitarian crisis, for example, and feel compelled to get involved. Here's how a quick version of how the Savvy Do Gooder process might go in that case:

1. 15 minutes: Ask yourself if this is an issue you really want to focus on.
    a. How is it relevant to your life and experience?
    b. How much do you know about it?
    c. Will the urge to get involved you're feeling right now still be there next week? Next month?
2. 1 hour: Google it.
    a. Read a couple of articles/blog posts about the issue.
    b. Find at least 2 different arguments about how to address it.

c. Find at least 2 different organizations working on it besides the one that originally brought it to your attention.
3. 1 hour: Research the organization(s).
   a. Visit the websites of at least 2 different organizations you're considering supporting.
   b. Check to see if they're legitimately registered charities.
   c. Google each of them to see if there's any third party commentary on the way they do business.
   d. Check them out on one of the charity-evaluation websites.
   e. See if you can answer the 5 Questions for each.
   f. Pick the one that looks like the best fit for you.
4. 15 minutes: Make the gift.
   a. Give online, write a cheque, etc.
5. 30 minutes (1 month later): Follow up
   a. Have they sent you a receipt?
   b. Have they sent any info about how your gift will be used?
   c. If not, call and bring it to their attention.
6. 30 minutes (1 year later): Review the relationship
   a. What, if any, additional info and requests have they sent you?
   b. How is it going from your perspective? Have they met the expectations you had when you gave? Are your goals for doing good being met?
7. 30 minutes: Either renew your gift or discontinue your giving.
   a. Consider communicating with the organization about; why you're giving again; questions you have; changes you'd like to suggest, or; why you've chosen not to give again.

There you have it – a grand total of 4 hours, spread out over a year. The initial steps can be accomplished in a single evening. Does that seem a bit more manageable?

If it still sounds like too much, consider asking yourself why you can't find the time to do even a basic version of savvy giving: might it be because your plate is full enough already? Many people feel that charitable giving is mandatory, even if they are so busy with day-to-day life that they can barely find the time to write a cheque; never mind becoming informed about the good they're trying to do.

You don't have to give to charity

This business of feeling like we have to give to charity is really unfortunate. Charity serves a purpose in our society, but (I can't stress this enough) it's not the only way to do good. If you feel like you simply haven't got the time or energy to follow the Savvy Do Gooder formula for giving to charity on top of all your other commitments, maybe there's a good reason for that. Maybe you're accomplishing a lot of good already.

Let's take a look at some of the things that might make us too busy to invest a lot of time in our charitable giving choices:

- Parenting: raising healthy, happy children is one of the most noble and positive contributions you can make to the world. This includes working hard to support them financially. Celebrate that as doing good.

- Work: if you are engaged in a career that makes a genuinely positive difference in the world (this doesn't have to be charitable work) and you are pouring all you've got into it, that's a noble and positive contribution to the world. Celebrate that as doing good.

- Lifestyle: if you make choices (like growing your own food or researching the sources of your clothing) to reduce the negative impact you have on the world, and these choices take more of your money, time, and energy than more conventional ones, that's a noble and positive contribution to the world. Celebrate that as doing good.

- Relationships: nurturing family relationships, helping out neighbours, participating in social activities, etc., are healthy behaviours that ultimately reduce the burden on formal social safety nets. Celebrate that as doing good.

- Health: if you spend time and energy treating your body as a temple, investing in exercise and diet to prevent physical and mental ailments now and in the future, you're likely to be less of a drain on governmental and charitable health care services now and in the future. Celebrate that as doing good.

This list could go on, but the point is: giving to charity is not the only way to accomplish good.

In fact, I would argue that's it's more important to invest in making sure the basic building blocks of our lives (family, work, lifestyle, health, etc.) are in good shape before giving to charity. Charity exists, in part, to pick up the pieces when these things fail. We should work on making them work first, and think about charity second. Otherwise, we run a higher risk of needing charitable help ourselves at some point.

If the commitments you already have in your life leave you too little time to follow the Savvy Do Gooder model of charitable giving, ask yourself: are you already doing good through those very commitments?

And if you are doing as much good as you can already, why beat yourself up over not being able to also give to charity properly? Despite what ads and fundraisers and well-intentioned charity volunteers say all the time, it's not mandatory to give. In fact, you're probably already giving quite a bit – whether you write a cheque to a charity or not.

Don't be fooled, don't "just give"

The common narrative around charity is false advertising, in my opinion. "Just give", they say. Someone is always coming up with a simpler, faster way to get the money from your pocket into those of charities. One click on a website – so easy! Just text a certain word to a certain number! Just drop your change in the jar at the checkout counter! "It's easy to make a difference", they say.

The truth is, we're being sold a bill of goods. Making it easier to hand over the cash does not make it easier to make a difference. The monetary transaction is not where the good is really done. Has the difficulty level of writing a cheque ever stopped you from giving to something you really believed in? No. It's a made-up problem, and we're being offered solutions to it as a way to pressure us into giving.

You can't blame the fundraisers, really – for years, "dollars raised" has been the primary measure of success in charity. Charities are accountable for reaching financial targets, above all else. More money is equated with more good. Most of the time, concrete results aren't even measured, never mind reported. Charities aren't made accountable for getting results – just for raising money and spending an acceptable percentage of it on things that sound like good ideas.

Is it any wonder that we now live in a culture where we're expected to give, give, give? Where the strong and pervasive message is that if you don't give, you're a bad person, no matter what else you do or don't do in your life? Is it any wonder that we're judged based on the quantity of our giving, not the quality?

Some of the greatest minds of the past 2 centuries – Warren Buffet, Steve Jobs, Bill Gates, Andrew Carnegie – have recognized that it's much harder to give money away properly than it is to make it. They're right - giving mindlessly can do more harm than good, as in the example of the African t-shirt giveaway from Chapter 4.

So why should we buy this mass-marketed philosophy that any charitable giving is better than none? That as long as we're forking over the cash, we're doing good? We shouldn't.

We have to recognize that our choice is not simply between giving and not giving – we actually have three choices: savvy giving, mindless giving, and not giving. We have to accept that not giving is a valid choice (a better one than mindless giving), and respect people's right to make it.

The rise of the Savvy Do Gooder

Doing good is not a one-shot deal. It's a lifelong experience. Problems and issues are ongoing, constantly evolving, and endlessly complex. We will never be 'done'. And really – isn't that for the best? If we solved all of the problems in the world, what would we do next?

Life would be awfully boring without challenges. Working to make the world a better place is, after all, one of the things that make life worth living. It's an adventure; pushing us to our limits, frustrating at times, and enormously rewarding when we win some small victory along the way.

I know that reading this book is probably not the first step on your do gooding journey, and it won't be the last. This book is not intended to make you into the perfect do-gooder; such a person doesn't exist! It doesn't claim to offer the only route to becoming savvy.

Neither does the advice offered here guarantee that you will never again be frustrated with the results of your giving, or the way a charity operates.

What I hope it does do for you is provide some food for thought and pointers about how to grow and improve in your efforts to do good. I hope it gives you a new perspective on your role, responsibilities, and rights within the process of making positive impact.

This whole 'do gooding' deal works best if we keep up a running commentary on it – lively dialogue about everything that has anything to do with getting good done. I believe that there are far too many sacred cows around doing good. Far too often, we're expected to take things on faith and blindly trust that they are being properly handled by someone else. Far too often, we allow 'doing good' and 'the rest of life' to be put into separate categories, as if they weren't all part and parcel of the same thing.

No more, I say! Let's argue, let's analyze, let's disagree and dissect and destroy and then rebuild! Let's build on the things that really work and get rid of the rest. Let's never stop working on it, tinkering with it, making it better.

Let's involve everyone in these discussions, from the donor to the charity professional to the professional corporate social responsibility officer to (last, but not least) the people we're trying to help. Let's create a space to publicly chew over everything that happens. In the age of social media, instant communication and virtual communities, this is more possible than ever before.

A Savvy Do Gooder is not a finished product. It's a person who is actively engaged in doing good, and in making the process of doing good work better.

The more Savvy Do Gooders are out there questioning, challenging, debating and improving, the better the system will work. Each in their own chosen issue area, these are the people who have the knowledge to recognize the good, the bad, and the ugly of do gooding efforts. They are the ones who are passionate and informed enough to speak out in favour of things that work, and against things that don't. They are vibrant, valuable, effective contributors to the change they want to see in the world. They never stop learning and they never stop growing. Join them.

I hope this book has given you some tools that help you in your quest to become one of these people. I hope something here has helped you as you work to make a difference in this world.

Most of all, I hope you're not done yet, and I look forward to seeing the wonders you accomplish. Good luck!

Acknowledgements

As I wrote this, my first book, help came from all directions – some expected, but many not. In the end, it came together thanks to:

- Linda Maul for her perspective and for seeing things in me I didn't know were there yet
- Kristen Cumming for having faith in me and providing some of the most constructive input I could ask for
- Paul Riopel for his living example and his editing skills
- Deanne Riopel for moral support and an unfailing willingness to come along on my learning journey
- Caitlin McElhone for her encouragement and invaluable feedback
- Tad Hargrave for his enthusiasm, guidance, and incredible foreword
- Karin Locke for her inspired cover design and layout wizardry
- Stephen Murgatroyd for planting the seed and paving the way
- Michelle, Megan, Patricia, Eugene, Colette, Vanessa, and a myriad of other friends and family for their support, friendship and input along the way

About the Author

Photo: Karin Locke

Nadine Riopel lives in Edmonton where, when she's not pondering how to make 'doing good' work better, she enjoys cooking, gardening, yoga, reading, walking, history, and the company of family and friends.